RACING BACK TO
VIETNAM

A JOURNEY IN WAR
AND PEACE

JOHN PENDERGRASS
U.S. AIR FORCE FLIGHT SURGEON

Improve your life. Change your world.

hatherleigh
Improve your life. Change your world.

Hatherleigh Press is committed to preserving and protecting the natural resources of the earth. Environmentally responsible and sustainable practices are embraced within the company's mission statement.

Visit us at www.hatherleighpress.com and register online for free offers, discounts, special events, and more.

Racing Back to Vietnam
Text Copyright © 2017 John Pendergrass

Library of Congress Cataloging-in-Publication Data is available.
ISBN: 978-1-57826-699-9

Printed in the United States

10 9 8 7 6 5 4 3 2 1

For the Americans
Killed, Wounded, or
Imprisoned during the
Vietnam War

"Each of us carried in his heart a separate war which in many ways was totally different, despite our common cause. We had different memories of people we'd known and the war itself, and we had different destinies in the postwar years."

"THE SORROW OF WAR," BAO NINH

CONTENTS

PART II: BACK TO VIETNAM

INTRODUCTION

HAVE YOU EVER been to an air show or a football game and watched fighter jets fly over the field in perfect formation? Three or four planes, barely a hundred feet above the ground, wings only a few feet apart. The aircraft arrive almost unexpectedly and quickly disappear into the distant horizon, leaving only the ear-splitting, deafening roar of jet engines hard at work. The whole thing happens in just a few seconds and nearly takes your breath away. The crowd's normal response is to stand awe-struck and break into applause. It's speed and power, sound and fury, the likes of which you've rarely seen before. You wish you could capture the moment, experience the thrill one more time.

I've had that feeling, and then some. For a year, I served as a United States Air Force flight surgeon at Da Nang Air Base, flying in the backseat of the workhorse fighter of the Vietnam War: the F-4 Phantom. The backseater served as the Weapon Systems Officer (WSO) and got an occasional chance to fly the aircraft. He was a junior partner in the F-4, a sidekick in the rear cockpit. The plane-driving, gun-shooting, bomb-dropping pilot in the front seat was the man in charge—the Aircraft Commander (AC). When it came to being shot down or killed, the two share the risk equally, true partners in every sense of the word.

Flying fighters is exhilarating. You are strapped into what seems like the fastest, most powerful machine ever made by man—the top aircraft in the Air Force's pecking order. Move the throttles far enough forward, and you can travel faster than the speed of sound. That authority and control are right there at your fingertips.

I learned on the job. I never went to pilot training and never attended navigator school; but I was able to come along for the ride in a Mach-2 fighter, a bit player in one of history's most intense and dangerous air wars.

I lived and flew with some of the best people in the world—the 390th Tactical Fighter Squadron, part of the 366th Tactical Fighter Wing. I knew next to nothing about flying, but my squadron welcomed me in and took me along. Thanks to their generosity, I experienced the adrenaline-rich, life-affirming euphoria of flying fighters in combat.

And what a ride it was. I flew 54 combat missions over South Vietnam, Laos, and Cambodia; we even dipped into North Vietnam on a few sorties. I survived anti-aircraft fire on multiple occasions, returning to base feeling more alive than when I took off, anxious to go again. It was the great adventure of my life.

On other occasions, I laid helpless and afraid in my barracks, subject to the whims of chance as the Viet Cong launched nighttime rocket attacks on our base. When the rockets came, there was little you could do except hunker down and hope that it wasn't your time. It was the capriciousness and unpredictability of the rocket attacks that were the most unsettling. Sometimes, a few incoming rounds were fired, and that was it; it was over. Other times, the attack seemed to go on for half the night. At Da Nang, it was known as "rolling dice with the Devil." You were at the mercy of the Viet Cong, and the best you could hope for was to break even.

Flying was just one part of my Vietnam experience. Most of my time was spent in my primary role as a physician, taking care of injured soldiers, healthy pilots, enlisted men with venereal disease, airmen addicted to heroin, people with Post Traumatic Stress Disorder (PTSD), and anyone else who walked through the doors of our medical dispensary.

It seemed as though I lived in two different worlds. In one, I flew fighters; in the other, I took care of sick people. I had friends and colleagues in both places, but the worlds rarely intersected.

I spent enough time in Vietnam to see the war as one of random deaths and hollow victories; a place where victory seemed indistinguishable from defeat. But I had learned long ago that this was often the nature of war. I was glad to have served and happy to depart with my honor intact, full of gratitude and relief.

I came home in late April 1972, just as Operation Linebacker, the final air assault on North Vietnam, was beginning. For most of my tour, the rules of engagement had kept North Vietnam off limits. The U.S.'s goal was no longer one of total victory; now, it was simply peace with honor. Everything changed in May 1972, when my squadron mates began flying over North Vietnam, the most heavily defended country in the world. While they were "going Downtown" (as flying over Hanoi was known), I was going back to the USA.

Like most of America, I was anxious to put the Vietnam War behind me. Since President Nixon had assured us that he was turning things over to the South Vietnamese, most of our country had long since quit paying attention to Vietnam. I jumped back into civilian life, quick to let things go. With a wife, a son, and a residency in ophthalmology, I had little time for reflection. I cried when the American prisoners of war (POWs) came home in early 1973. These were men I identified with: the vast majority of them were pilots and backseaters captured when their fighter aircraft were shot down over North Vietnam. These POWs were my heroes, and their fate was always on my mind.

The end, when it came, came very quickly. In 1975, the South Vietnamese government collapsed, and the war was over. I tried not to think of the men in my squadron who died, or of the more than fifty-eight thousand Americans who lost their life in the war, or of the hundreds of thousands of our South Vietnamese allies whose fates were now in the hands of the North Vietnamese. I tried not to dwell on the tragedy, the heroism, the absurdity of war. Like most of America, I was anxious to put it behind me.

Forty-five years after I first arrived, I'll be returning to Vietnam in order to participate in the Ironman 70.3 triathlon held at Da Nang. The idea seems appealing—a new challenge for an old man. At the time of my service in Vietnam, the sport of triathlon hadn't even been invented. It wasn't until 1974 that someone thought of linking swimming, biking, and running—in that order—to create a single event; it was another four years before the Ironman brand was created.

This is my chance to return to Southeast Asia under more idyllic conditions. There will be no rocket attacks, no anti-aircraft fire; I'll be able to relax in the sunshine and swim in the sea; a septuagenarian's spring break, of sorts.

In reality, the triathlon idea is just an excuse to return to Vietnam; to go back into my youth, to touch the past. These journeys back in time seem much more attractive when you reach retirement age. When you are in your thirties or forties, you are living in "real time;" there's little to go back to. Life is lived forward and understood backwards. Besides, I had already completed six Ironman triathlons on six continents in my sixties, and truthfully, I felt like I had ridden that horse as far as it could go.

Plus, the number of Ironman triathlons has only increased over the last decade, with races now being held in every corner of the globe. When enough people have done something, the value of it changes. Ironman had lost its capacity to inspire me; it was no longer special, it was just another endurance event.

At least, that's what I told myself. In truth, my lack of enthusiasm was probably due to the fact that my ideal window for doing a triathlon had closed over thirty years ago. Nowadays, I still have grand goals—the mind never quits dreaming—but my schemes are based more on wishful thinking than on reality. My body refuses to cooperate. I'm in my eighth decade of life, and nothing physical comes easy at this age. My aches and pains can usually be held in check by a fistful of medications, but there are many days that I feel like an old man who made a wrong turn on his way to the nursing home.

My journey to Vietnam is inspired by a mixture of nostalgia and reflection. Since memories can get lost in the clutter of time, I've made a concerted effort to recapture my year in Southeast Asia. I've read through the over one hundred and fifty letters that I wrote my wife and mother from Vietnam; I've studied my flight records searching for clues; I know the date and duration of each mission and the tail number of the aircraft (though little else, admittedly). I've attended several recent reunions of my fighter wing and skimmed through dozens of history books giving various takes on the Vietnam War. In truth, I feel I know more about Vietnam now than I did during my tour.

I'm anxious to return to Da Nang, the country's third largest city. I'll be landing on the very same runway I departed from forty-five years ago. During the war, it was the busiest airport in the world. I can still clearly remember leaving Da Nang at the end of my tour; it was one of the greatest moments of my life. I'll never forget the joy, the exhilaration, the applause when our "freedom bird" took off in April 1972.

It has been nearly forty-five years. I saw Vietnam in wartime, and I was happy to leave it behind. But I know the country has changed dramatically nearly half a century. I am anxious to go back to Southeast Asia. Most of all, I want to talk to the people of Vietnam. Even though the vast majority were born after the war's end, surely there must be a few who have a direct memory of the conflict.

What do today's Vietnamese really think of that era they call the "American War"? This is a voyage of rediscovery that I'm eager to begin.

1

LIFE IN DANANG

SOUTHEAST ASIA DURING
THE VIETNAM WAR

ONE

AHEAD OF SCHEDULE

May 30, 1971

MY FIRST DAY in Vietnam was one of the worst days of my life.

After begging, scheming, and conspiring, I'd somehow managed to get my boots on the ground on the very last day of the month, two days ahead of my scheduled arrival. As a result, I was able to avoid paying federal income tax on most of my salary for the entire month of May.

I made a bad choice. I managed to beat the Internal Revenue Service out of few dollars of taxes in exchange for surviving a Viet Cong attack on my very first day at war.

At the time, arriving in Vietnam a few days early seemed like a rational move. Uncle Sam had decided that any officer who spent a single day a month "in country" could exclude roughly $500 of his pay from federal income tax; enlisted personnel could exempt their entire paycheck for that month. Not only that, a single day in country earned you a full month of combat pay. Slipping into a combat zone on the final day of the month became a well-established strategy during the war. Many of the big brass stationed all over the Far East would fly to Vietnam on the last day of the month, have a few drinks at the officer's club, and fly out the next day, all the while exempting two months of pay from federal taxes—as well as qualifying for combat pay.

I'd finished Jungle Survival School (JSS) at Clark Air Base in the Philippines around May 27, and had a few days to burn before I was scheduled to arrive at Da Nang. Tom, my medical school roommate, was serving as a flight surgeon at Clark and offered to show me the country. We discussed spending a couple of days in Manila, relaxing and seeing the sights before I headed off to the war. But I was poor and knew that money is hard to come by, so I decided to skip the tour of the Philippines and try to get to Vietnam by May 30 in order to get my income tax exemption and combat pay.

Only two years out of medical school, I was just a few dollars shy of broke. I had a young family, a load of debt, and a growing dislike of the IRS. For most of my life I had been too poor to notice, but the last couple of Aprils I had been forced to pay up for taxes due, and I was none too happy about it.

Now, as a captain in the Air Force, I was making more money than I ever had in my life. My monthly paycheck, which included flight pay, medical pay, and combat pay, topped out around $1,000. I was doing my best to get my financial feet on the ground and was anxious to hold on to every single dollar that I could.

Arriving in Vietnam ahead of schedule was one of the easiest things I'd ever done. I hustled over to the air terminal at Clark to plead my case. While there were numerous flights daily between the Philippines and Vietnam, all with plenty of empty seats, my request was a little confusing for the sergeant at the scheduling desk. After all, I was trying to leave the Philippines early to *go* to Vietnam, while most folks were trying to get *out* of Vietnam and spend a few days in the Philippines. I showed him my orders, explained that they really needed me at Da Nang, and told him that I was ready to serve my country. He smiled, shook his head, shuffled some papers, and the next morning I was in the air and on the way to my new home in Southeast Asia.

On the flight over, I thought of my wife and eight-month-old son back in Mississippi. I was starting a twelve-month tour on the other side of the planet, far away from the people I loved, fighting a war I had largely ignored as I worked my way through college, medical school, and an internship. I had always supported the war in principle but, until now, had had little skin in the game.

By and large, the people of the South, even in 1971, were pro-military. There were relatively few anti-war demonstrations and even fewer draft dodgers. My local newspaper listed servicemen and casualties from our area, but only a few of my friends had served in Vietnam. Most had muddled their way through college and grad school; some profited from a bad knee or fallen arches; a few managed to join the National Guard.

All of that changed for me in the spring of 1971. Not only was I destined to spend a full year away from my family and home, I had drawn the worst assignment in the U.S. Air Force. Everyone told me the same thing—if you have to go on an unaccompanied tour of Southeast Asia, make sure it's one of the bases in Thailand. It's a warm and welcoming country, with wonderful food and lovely women. Many of the combat missions in Vietnam flew out of Thai air bases. Udorn, Ubon, Takhli, Korat, Nakhon Phanom—even today, the names have a musical, mythical ring; a hint of the tropics. Granted, the combat missions were just as dangerous if you flew from Thailand, but you were returning to the beautiful, peaceful Thai countryside instead of war-torn South Vietnam. Plus, none of the bases in Thailand ever got attacked by Viet Cong.

The difference in assignments was obvious; a lot of civilians paid good money to go on holiday in Thailand, but no one vacationed in Vietnam.

Of course, if you *had* to be stationed in Vietnam, Tan Son Nhut Air Base was the place to be. The base is next door to Saigon, the "Paris of the Orient," the dynamic cultural center of Vietnam—a city where every sin was available for a price. Saigon was the headquarters for the U.S. war effort, meaning that everyone from generals to civilian contractors to journalists, do-gooders, and other big shots called the city home. None of them were accustomed to doing without.

The same could not be said of Da Nang.

My previous nine months in the Air Force were spent with the 1st Special Operations Wing at Hurlburt Field in Fort Walton Beach, a pleasant Florida community full of white beaches, seafood restaurants, and military retirees pursuing the good life. No one worked hard at Hurlburt; the base pretty much shut down on the weekend. My family had finally gotten a spot with on-base housing; our hardest job was deciding which seafood restaurant to eat at.

One day, while I was seeing patients at the dispensary (and planning my next SCUBA diving trip), I received a call from a sergeant in personnel. I knew him as a patient, and he was very apologetic, almost contrite, as he gave me the grim news: "Sir, I've just received your orders for a permanent change of assignment to Da Nang Air Base, Republic of Vietnam."

I felt like I had been punched in the gut. I had hoped to exit the military unscathed, but a month later I was gone from Florida. After a too-quick farewell week in San Francisco with my wife, Polly, I was on a military charter out of Travis Air Force Base in California, headed to Jungle Survival School (JSS) in the Philippines.

Everyone in the USAF who flew in combat in Southeast Asia attended JSS. For nearly a week, you would focus on learning how to survive and be rescued if you're shot down. At the time, I had no idea how much I would be able to fly during my year at Da Nang, but I knew the world of fighters was a risky one.

I was glad to have the opportunity to attend JSS. Search and rescue is a deadly serious business, and I paid close attention to everything I was told. Much of the training dealt with survival and rescue gear; items like radios, flares, and parachutes, the equipment that would help keep you alive if you were shot down.

Probably the most important thing we practiced was calling in the HH-53 rescue helicopter, the Super Jolly Green Giant. These mammoth green choppers, the final link in the Search and Rescue (SAR) mission, pulled hundreds of downed airmen to safety during the Vietnam War.

It was an interesting exercise. If you are shot down, the Jolly Green has to pinpoint your location in order to pick you up. As the chopper flies overhead, you direct it via your radio on the correct direction to turn: "Turn right thirty degrees, back left ten degrees." It's sort of like a game of "hot and cold." You talk back and forth with the Jolly Green and, once he has a fix on your position, you activate your rescue flare ("pulling your smoke"). A large plume of smoke shoots into the sky, the chopper hovers overhead and lowers the jungle penetrator, a large cable with three arms on the end folded inward that is designed to break through the jungle canopy. You let the boom hit the ground, unfold the arms, fasten the sling, take a seat, grip the cable firmly with both hands, and away you go, up into the sky.

We practiced in an open area rather than a triple canopy jungle, and everyone got to take a turn. The whole experience was new and different, rising into the heavens (though it was probably little more than twenty yards), holding on for dear life, hoping this was the only time you would ever have to do this. I could tell the Jolly Green crew was a little bored, even annoyed. Those men are genuine heroes, and this was a humdrum, tedious routine for them.

Needless to say, JSS is staged in a jungle. Now, I like the outdoors, and I grew up in small town Mississippi, but the only jungle I had ever seen was in Tarzan movies. The hills around Clark AFB were the real thing: pristine, unadulterated jungle that looked as if no one had visited in centuries. Tall canopy forests, a lot of vines, plenty of strange insects, near constant animal noises, the works.

The prevailing wisdom at JSS was that there's plenty of food and water in the jungle...if you know where to search. I wasn't sure I believed that, and I hoped I didn't have to find out. We received briefings on what to eat and, in a few cases, what to never, *ever* eat. In the jungles of Southeast Asia, there were quite a few things that would kill you if you ate them. Everyone received a deck of cards with the various plants and their names pictured in bold green colors. Of course, no one seemed to take the deck of cards very seriously; it's hard enough to memorize the names of foreign plants, and it wasn't very practical to take along a deck of cards when you flew.

The jungle itself wasn't the only danger that downed airmen faced. If you were unfortunate enough to be shot down in Southeast Asia, you also had to know how to hide and evade the enemy until you could (hopefully) be rescued. For that reason, the JSS employed local Negrito tribesmen to teach evasion and survival skills. These short, dark-skinned aborigines had lived in the jungle for centuries. Reported to be loyal resistance fighters during the World War II Japanese occupation, the Negritos around Clark Air Base were accorded special privileges.

Whenever we were in the jungle, the Negritos would be hanging around, squatting silently and safely away from any Americans. They spoke little English, and no one seemed to speak their dialect, but they always seemed to be aware of what was going on. The Negritos knew the jungle, and they were part of the great game we played each morning. Each of us was given a small marker or chit to carry in our pockets. We were sent into the jungle with a one hour head start, ahead of the Negritos. The object was to hide and avoid detection until mid-day. If the Negrito trackers found you, you had to surrender your chit without complaint. Each capture meant that the Negritos were a bag of rice richer.

My strategy was simple. I headed out into the jungle at a brisk jog, carrying nothing but a couple of flasks of water. I felt that if I put a lot of distance behind me I could hide successfully while the Negrito trackers searched closer to home. I figured that even though the Negritos knew the jungle well, they would still need time to check the various hiding spots.

There were no signs in the jungle, no roads, not even anything I'd call a well-worn path. I had run for nearly an hour when it occurred to me that I might have been better off putting as much effort in hiding as I had in running.

I found a good tree with thick foliage. In reality, the jungle is full of "good trees;" what made this tree appealing were the sturdy, low-lying limbs that let me climb fifteen feet into the air. I settled on my perch, sipped my last bit of water, congratulated myself on being lord of the jungle, and waited for a couple of hours to pass before I emerged triumphantly from my hiding spot.

Less than twenty minutes later, a pair of Negritos dressed in cut-off shorts, old tee shirts, and worn out sneakers came gliding past silently. They went twenty yards in the opposite direction, stopped, turned around, and came back to my tree. The pair looked up, grinned, and whispered, "Chit, chit, come, come." I climbed down and handed over my chit. With one man in front of me and one behind, they led me back to the starting point.

I had spent sixty minutes running away, but it took only twenty minutes of walking to get home. I must have spent a lot of time running in circles. I could tell that surviving in the jungle wasn't one of my strong points; I hoped I never had to use these evasion skills in Vietnam.

Da Nang Air Base was everything I'd expected: hot, humid, and loud. My new home was the epicenter of the air war in Southeast Asia, the busiest airport in the world—a land of barbed wire and sandbags, living from one disaster to the next. F-4 Phantoms flew around the clock and the smell of jet fuel seemed to linger in the air. There were no grass lawns and no trees, just ugly weeds lining the ditches. Save for the runways, the base had the impermanence of a movie set. Most of the buildings were prefabricated modular units that had been added as the war grew and grew. The whole complex was surrounded by twin security fences, separated by a heavily mined no-man's land with guard posts manned by South Vietnamese soldiers.

As I left the plane, already sweating profusely, an enlisted man helped carry one of my duffel bags. "Damn, Doc," he said, "did you bring a load of bricks to Vietnam?"

If you're on flying status, you're granted an extra hundred pounds of luggage, and I had used every ounce of my allowance. Since I would be starting my ophthalmology residency when my tour at Da Nang was done, I had brought along many of my textbooks to study. I was probably the first person to bring his library with him to the Vietnam War.

Because I had arrived a few days ahead of schedule, there was no one at the arrival terminal to welcome me to Vietnam, no one to tell me what to do or where to go. I got on the phone, called my squadron, introduced myself, and told them I needed a lift. A short ride later, I was at my squadron headquarters, my new home for the next twelve months.

The sign on the front said "390th Tactical Fighter Squadron" and featured a large oval plaque with a wild boar's head. The boar was dark brown with wild-looking eyes and menacing tusks. The 390th was one of three F-4 Phantom squadrons that made up the 366th Tactical Fighter Wing (TFW), known as the Gunfighters.

The Gunfighter name struck a chord with me. It seemed like a good name for a fighter wing; it had a Wild West aura, a certain panache, sort of like the shootout at the OK Corral.

Of course, I soon learned that the Gunfighter name was due to the wing's success with a 20 mm external mounted gun pod. Early F-4 models were forced to rely on radar-guided or heat-seeking missiles in aerial combat. The nose gun was a welcome addition for dogfights as well as for close air support of ground troops.

Later, I found out there was a little more to the name. It turned out that part of the impetus for the Gunfighter tag came from a rivalry between two Air Force wings. The 8th TFW in Ubon, Thailand was led by one of the greatest fighter pilots of all time, Colonel Robin Olds. Known as the "Wolfpack" and headed by the dashing, charismatic Olds, the 8th TFW seemed to garner all the publicity. In May 1967, the month with the most air-to-air engagements during the entire Rolling Thunder campaign, the 366th TFW (my new wing) had scored one more aerial victory than the 8th TFW, but didn't get as much attention in the media as the Wolfpack. It was determined that what the 366th TFW needed to catch the public's eye was a label that people could remember; a name, not a number. Thus, the Gunfighter moniker was born.

The squadron barracks, or hootch as they were sometimes known, looked a lot like a low-class college dorm; a little basic, but not bad at all for wartime. Each room had two single beds, a couple of desks, wall-mounted closets, and linoleum floors. My bed had linen, a blanket, a pillow, a flak-jacket, and a steel helmet; all in all, not the usual recipe for a good night's sleep. A small window about the size of a loaf of bread let in a glimmer of sunlight, and an air conditioner that rattled mercilessly was anchored beneath the window. A basic bathroom and shower was shared by two rooms. And, since in the vernacular of wartime I was an FNG (a "F—ing New Guy") I drew a second floor room with a dying air conditioner.

The two-story barracks were sandbagged on the outside up to around six feet in height. The outside of the top floor was bare, with no sandbag protection. The walls seemed barely thick enough to stop someone with a slingshot. I mentioned this sandbag deficiency to some of the other guys, but no one seemed concerned. In retrospect, I understand their attitude; this was my first day in Vietnam, and I was complaining about a lack of sandbags to men who were getting shot at over the Ho Chi Minh Trail. I kept my mouth shut and hoped a room on the ground floor would open up.

Soon it was late afternoon, and after unpacking, I walked down to the medical dispensary, the spot where I would spend most of my working days. The 366th Tactical Fighter Wing was the main occupant of Da Nang Air Base, and was, in fact, the reason for the base's existence. As a result, the Gunfighter theme extended to the rest of the base. The entrance to our medical complex had a sign that said, "366th Dispensary, the Germfighters." *What could be better?* I thought; I was going to be a Gunfighter and a Germfighter at the same time.

If I had walked a few blocks further, I would have found the base chapel, home of the "Sinfighters." The military chaplains were there to help with the myriad of spiritual and social problems that arise in wartime. Everyone knows that Satan never takes a holiday, and the same can be said for the war. Since the conflict ran seven days a week, around the clock, the chaplains would post a sign in the front of the chapel on the Sabbath that read, "Today is Sunday."

Upon reaching the dispensary, one of the other flight surgeons took me around and introduced me to everyone at the dispensary. There were two or three other flight surgeons and three or four general medical officers on the staff. In addition to flying, the flight surgeons took care of the pilots and navigators, removing them from flying status when they were ill and clearing them to return to the air when they were well. Otherwise, a flight surgeon's medical duties are much the same as a general medical officer. We had a lot in common: we were all just a year or two removed from an internship, not yet trained in a specialty, and used to long hours of work.

Oh, and one other thing: no one had volunteered to serve at Da Nang.

Everyone seemed glad to see me, appreciative of an extra hand to share the work, sympathetic for a man just starting a year-long journey, and happy to share insights on what to expect at Da Nang.

When you first arrive at a new assignment, you are constantly meeting new people. Most of the other physicians were friendly and curious. We learned about each other's family, friends, training, and future plans. A common theme was, "How in the hell did we end up here?" Few physicians ever joined the Air Force with plans to come to Vietnam.

One or two of the people I met barely seemed to catch my name. Since I was a late arrival and they were scheduled to rotate home soon, I was a mere blip on the screen. It wasn't worth their time or effort to befriend me, as they would soon be gone. These men were "short;" in other words, they were not long for the world of Southeast Asia.

Everyone sent to Vietnam served a twelve-month tour. If you arrived on a certain day, your date of estimated return from overseas (DEROS) was one year later. Time worked backwards; days of the week had no meaning in wartime, only the number of days until your DEROS, hence the Sinfighter's Sunday sign. Everyone had their DEROS tattooed on their brain. It was the most important date in the world. You might forget your wedding anniversary, but you never lost track of your DEROS.

That night, I laid in bed, tired and a little depressed. I was the longest man in all of Vietnam; twelve months seemed like an eternity. The food at the mess hall was so bad that I could barely eat it. The troops eating field rations out in the jungle probably would have loved it, but I could barely keep it down. I really missed my wife and nine-month-old son, John.

My first day in country set the tone for my entire time in Vietnam. For nearly a year, I was under-loved and underfed, the worst curses that any man can suffer.

I laid in bed, brooding; a year to go in this distant corner of the globe, no family and food unfit for a dog. Self-pity flowed like a river. How could it possibly get any worse?

It all began in the middle of the night. For a moment, I thought I was having a bad dream. Loud explosions rang out, the ground shook and rumbled, search lights and flares lit the sky, sirens wailed. A disembodied voice came over the loudspeaker confirming the obvious: "Da Nang is under attack."

The rockets came both singly and in groups. The attack would seem to be over, and then a latecomer would explode, an afterthought of some inconsiderate Viet Cong.

Welcome to Rocket City.

During the Vietnam War, Da Nang was attacked nearly a hundred times. Early on, there had been sappers and mortars, but now it was mostly rockets. I was well aware of Da Nang's reputation. Before I'd arrived, I'd tried to learn something about rockets; I'd even tried to read a book about them, but I gave up after a few pages. The book was of little help to me; it seemed like a manual for people with engineering degrees.

Everything I actually learned about rockets I learned from talking to other people at Da Nang. Everyone had a story to share; legends and myths blended in with facts. Apparently, most of the rockets being used were 122 mm Russian-made weapons with a range of several miles. Since launch sites were subject to retaliatory artillery or air strikes, the rockets were set up on earthen ramps with a timer to delay the launch, allowing the Viet Cong to safely escape.

The main targets were the barracks, fuel storage areas, bomb dumps, and aircraft. By the time I arrived at Da Nang, most of the aircraft were parked in concrete revetments safely out of harm's way. The people were less well-protected. Six weeks after I arrived, a rocket hit an enlisted men's barracks, killing five and wounding thirty-eight. The whole experience of rocket attacks had a Russian roulette quality to it. Since an air base has a lot of open space, the rockets would sometimes only make a big hole in the ground or a crater in one of the runways, something that could be repaired in a few hours. Other times, they caused death and destruction.

I'm no warrior; I was scared as hell. Only a fool would be optimistic in a spot like that. My instinct to stay alive was strong, but what could I do? Pretend it wasn't happening? Hope it would go away? Drop down on my knees in prayer? I knew this wasn't the siege at Khe Sanh and it wasn't the Marines battling at Hue, but it felt real enough to me.

It was a bad beginning to a long year. On my first night in Vietnam, I was cooped up in my non-air conditioned room, sweating in my underwear, blaming myself for leaving JSS ahead of schedule and cursing the IRS for enticing me to an early trip to a combat zone. I slipped on my flak jacket, strapped on my steel helmet, and cuddled up in the corner in the fetal position. It was impossible to think of sleep while wearing a helmet and flak jacket; real grunts in the field may do it, but that's not me. I was never cut out to be an infantryman. The terror of waiting out an artillery or rocket attack isn't like flying fighters—you can't dodge, and there's no skill involved. If a rocket has your name on it, you're done. I lay there wondering how many ways a man can be afraid.

As I laid in bed, waiting for my number to come up, my roommate twisted a little bit, made some noises that didn't really seem human, and rolled back over. I wondered if I should wake him and tell him to put on his gear. But I was the new guy, and I didn't know my barracks buddy very well. *Is there etiquette for rocket attacks?* I wondered. *Wake me only if you think I might be killed or injured?*

As I lay in bed, trying to remind myself that when something can't go on forever, it *will* eventually stop, I eventually dozed a little, and before long, the morning sun was peeking through the window.

At Da Nang, the rockets always came at night. I grew to love the light of dawn. I got out of bed with only 364 days left to go in country.

My hour had not yet come.

It all seemed grossly unfair. My arrival at Da Nang must have been badly timed, I thought. I had assumed that when you reported for war, you were given a grace period, a freshman orientation, a honeymoon of sorts, before the fighting began. Being shot at was an abstract concept that I wasn't prepared to confront, much less deal with. For me, my first night in Vietnam had veered toward the apocalyptic. The best that could be said was that I was a wealthier man due to my early arrival in country. A solid $500 of income saved from the greedy claws of the IRS, plus an extra month of combat pay.

This wasn't the last time someone would try to kill me in Vietnam. I hoped that in the future, I could muster up a little more courage than I had shown my first day at war.

TWO

WHY VIETNAM?

April 1971

A COUPLE OF weeks before I left Hurlburt Field to head to Vietnam, I was scheduled to attend a mandatory briefing for all airmen being sent to Southeast Asia. This was the final send-off for the troops, and the families of the men being deployed were urged to attend the meeting. Polly was busy packing and tending to our eight-month-old son, John, so my mother, down for one last visit before I shipped out, tagged along with me.

This briefing was just another box to check; one of the many things you do before being sent on a combat assignment. I had gotten all the right kinds of vaccinations, qualified as an expert with a .38 revolver, gotten a flight line driver's license, obtained a top secret security clearance, and drawn up a last will and testament. Now, I was going to learn why we were fighting in Vietnam.

The briefing wasn't a bad idea, on paper. Although the war had been going on a good six years, many Americans still had little or no knowledge of where Vietnam was located on the globe, much less about its history or culture. For most people, Southeast Asia was a collection of countries that were difficult to tell apart.

By 1971, the glory and innocence of the early days of the Vietnam conflict were gone. The war was a stalemate; both sides were claiming victory, but only the losses were real. More than fifty thousand Americans had died, and there weren't a lot of war-hungry hawks left (at least, not among those of us chosen to do the fighting). The public still supported the troops on principle, but the conflict itself had been disowned by virtually every segment of society. It had turned into a war without end or purpose. I certainly wasn't thrilled to be leaving my family to spend a year in Vietnam, but I hoped I could serve honorably and be as good as the people around me.

My mother and I arrived at the meeting place, one of those sterile, interchangeable concrete block buildings that populate Air Force bases across the United States. We found a seat in a room with a couple of dozen or so airmen, both enlisted men and officers, and their families.

Everyone received a copy of a sixty-four page full-color magazine entitled "Mission Vietnam," produced by the Seventh Air Force. (This was the era of the popular Sunday night television series *Mission: Impossible*. I loved *Mission: Impossible*, but I wasn't sure I felt the same about "Mission Vietnam.")

I still have my copy of "Mission Vietnam." The cover shows an F-4 Phantom taking off at dusk, headed toward the setting sun. The red warning lights on the wings and tail glow gently in the dark, but the twin afterburners look like exploding comets. I knew I was assigned to an F-4 squadron, so the color photo had a certain sparkle and wonder, a glimpse of exciting things to come.

The briefing was conducted by a couple of lieutenant colonels flown in from Washington, DC. They looked a bit out of place in their blue dress uniforms with their chests full of ribbons. (Florida, like Vietnam, is always hot, and everyone wore either khakis, fa-

tigues, or a flight suit year around; no one wore their decorations.)
The colonels took us on a slow and deliberate march through the
history of Vietnam. The Chinese communists were an important
ally of the North Vietnamese during the Vietnam War, but this
was an exception to the historical trend. Trapped by geography
on the edge of a vast empire, the Vietnamese had been battling
their Chinese neighbors for centuries. That ill will even persists
today, with both countries claiming sovereignty over the Paracel
and Spratly Islands in the South China Sea.

The Portuguese showed up in the early sixteenth century, followed a hundred years later by the Dutch. The French came next,
in the mid-nineteenth century, hoping to save souls and make
money. French colonialism was brutal and merciless. The *colons*,
as the French settlers were known, brought the fruits of Western
civilization to Indochina, but the natives saw little of the benefits.
The locals worked in the lowest echelons of the civil service with
no chance of self-government. A large influx of Chinese merchants
arriving around the same time helped ensure that the Vietnamese
stayed on the bottom rung of society.

Serious resistance to French rule first arose in the early twentieth
century, led by the man later known as Ho Chi Minh. Ho attended
the Versailles Conference after the end of World War I to advocate
for Vietnamese independence. At the time, Ho was an unknown,
barely noticed by anyone at the conference, and the French quickly
resumed their colonial domination.

Looking for a route to independence, Ho hooked up with the
communists. One of the colonels repeatedly called him a "Mos-
cow-trained revolutionary" (an accusation that would send chills
down your spine during the height of the Cold War). The French
held on to Indochina until World War II, when the Japanese invaded the region, an area rich in natural resources critical for the
Japanese war machine.

The French folded early in the war under the Nazi blitzkrieg, leaving an opening in Vietnam. Ho founded an independence league known as the Viet Minh, and when the Japanese surrendered to the United States in 1945, Ho's forces declared independence and took control of the country. It was a very brief rule; Chinese troops entered Vietnam from the north, British troops came into the south, the Japanese troops were disarmed, and the country was handed back to the French.

The French effort to maintain control of Indochina, supported economically by the America, was one of the last gasps of colonialism. The United States, traditionally anti-colonial in outlook, was more interested in a stable, anti-communist French ally. What is now called the First Indochina War ended in 1954, when the French garrison at Dien Bien Phu fell to the Vietnamese general Vo Nguyen Giap.

There was a lot of pressure for the United States to rescue the French at Dien Bien Phu. Some pushed for nuclear weapons, an urging that President Eisenhower wisely resisted. Ike had learned a lesson that many subsequent presidents have failed to grasp: never get involved in a ground war in Asia.

The Geneva Accords in 1954 ended French involvement in Indochina and partitioned the country along the 17th parallel, with unification to be decided by an election at a later date. The south was led by Ngo Dinh Diem, a Catholic in a majority Buddhist country. Diem was a nationalist with no history of French collaboration. His government, with U.S. assistance, moved nearly a million Catholics from the North and their communist rulers to South Vietnam.

By this point in the colonels' history lesson, everyone in the room was getting a little antsy. Eyes were beginning to glaze over as the briefing dragged on like one of your children's piano recitals. The colonels took turns standing in front of the screen with a long pointer. They would tap the screen, someone somewhere would push a button, and another image or another table of statistics would appear on the screen. And so the lecture continued.

Shortly after his inauguration, President Kennedy began sending military advisors to help the South Vietnamese. Diem, his brother, and his infamous sister-in-law, Madame Nhu, proved to be weak, uninspiring leaders. Diem was overthrown in a coup and killed in November 1963, just three weeks before Kennedy was assassinated.

In August 1964, the USS *Maddox*, on patrol off the Vietnamese coast, was attacked on two occasions by enemy torpedo boats. Congress passed the Gulf of Tonkin Resolution, giving President Lyndon Johnson the authority to use conventional military force in Southeast Asia without a congressional declaration of war. (Although there is a serious question today as to whether the second attack on the *Maddox* was real, I don't recall any doubt at the time of the briefing.)

In March 1965, thirty-five hundred Marines waded ashore at Da Nang, my future home base. These first American combat units were sent to protect American planes. Six bloody years followed; the Rolling Thunder air campaign over North Vietnam; Khe Sanh; the Tet Offensive; the list goes on. Each day the evening news brought reports of more Americans killed in action. Often, the monthly totals reached into the hundreds.

President Nixon began withdrawing troops in 1969, turning the war over to the South Vietnamese, looking for "peace with honor"—a process called Vietnamization. With fewer U.S. ground troops, more of the burden fell on air power.

In the spring of 1971 as my mother and I sat through the briefing, I was more concerned with peace than with honor. There were fewer Americans in Vietnam than ever; even the anti-war crowd seemed a little exhausted, but there was no end in sight for the Vietnam War. There were on-and-off negotiations to end the war, but they didn't seem to have the same sense of urgency that I had.

I viewed the Vietnam War as an unwanted interruption in my life. I would have preferred to end my Air Force career on the beaches of Florida. I had a beautiful wife, a son, and an ophthalmology residency waiting for me twelve months down the road. I knew I had drawn a bad lot, but I felt I had to do the best job I could while trying to keep looking forward.

My mother, on the other hand, was a product of her times. A single parent who came of age during the Great Depression, she worked two jobs to support a family in the days before welfare, food stamps, and Medicaid. She had seen her two brothers go off to fight in World War II, watched as the Korean War evolved into a bloody stalemate, and followed the Cold War hot spots of Berlin and Cuba. Just five months earlier, her oldest son had died unexpectedly. Now her next son was headed off to war. Military service was an obligation her generation accepted; it was a price you paid to be an American.

She wasn't an expressive person. People of her generation could be loving and stoic at the same time. She always supported me and never interfered in my decisions. As we left the briefing, she shook her head and said, "This is a fight the Vietnamese need to decide. It isn't worth American lives."

She probably would have said much worse, but she didn't want to unnecessarily burden me. I'm sure she felt the great sadness and anxiety a parent feels when a child goes off to war. The old saying "You're only as happy as your unhappiest child" was as true then as it is today.

I headed back home to pack for Vietnam, enlightened but unconvinced.

THREE

GETTING MY FEET ON THE GROUND

June 5, 1971

A WEEK LATER, we had another rocket attack. It was the same scenario: middle of the night, explosions, sirens, flares, flak jackets, fear, and anger.

These attacks seemed to be part of life at Da Nang. The next day, everyone was talking about the rockets—how many struck the base, what was damaged, whether anyone was killed. Two days later, no one even mentioned them.

Most of my time was spent checking in, filling out forms, finding out where various offices were located, and listening with envy as people talked about how short they were, or where they are going for R and R. The whole world seemed to be headed home (or at least to Hawaii) while I was stuck at Da Nang. I'd gotten a DEROS calendar—a sketch of an F-4, scored into 365 parts, sort of like a paint-by-numbers portrait. I'd already colored in six days; only 359 more before I go back to the real world.

First, a few things about my new home. Da Nang has the same basic buildings as Air Force bases around the world. When the Marines first landed here in 1965, the base was little more than a primitive airfield, but the military had been steadily building for the last six years and the facilities had greatly improved. It was a healthy expansion; the civilian contractors grew rich, and life became easier at Da Nang. By 1971, everything was in place: personnel, mess halls, maintenance, security police, dispensary, and chapel, not to mention the aircraft and the men who flew and maintained them. Large blocks of barracks, vast areas of fuel dumps, and munitions storage were a big part of the war story, but I also found a good library and a movie theater, as well as a base exchange (BX).

By the standards back home, our BX would have qualified as a first-rate liquor and tobacco store. There wasn't a huge variety of brands, but the sheer volume of booze and smokes was impressive. Granted, the stuff was relatively cheap, and it had to be tightly controlled lest it end up on the local black market. This was a nearly impossible task; just a few blocks outside the base gates, you could find everything available at the BX and much more, including whiskey, drugs, women, and weapons. Everything had its price on the black market.

Every new arrival at Da Nang was issued a ration card. It was an egalitarian system, with enlisted men and officers of all ranks having the same limits. Each month, you could purchase three cases of beer, three bottles of wine, and three quarts of hard liquor. If you were a serious drinker and you needed more, you could borrow a friend's ration card and use his unused allotment. Not that there were many allotments going to waste; at Da Nang, some people drank to remember, some people drank to forget, but whatever the motivation, there were plenty of opportunities to imbibe.

Your ration card also entitled you to purchase a big item once a year, such as a camera or tape deck. But the selection for these items was meager, so most people preferred to get them by mail from the Pacific Exchange (PACEX) catalog. Cameras, tape decks, brass, ceramics, silk screens, and other items were ordered by mail and usually shipped directly home to the USA. I never got a handle on the value of goods from the East, but they must have been a good bargain; I got regular letters from my wife instructing me to order items for various friends and family members.

More than any helmet or M-16 rifle, these consumer goods are the artifacts of the Vietnam veteran. Even today, forty-five years later, I can visit someone's home and tell they served in Southeast Asia. The silk screens and brass have survived well; the cameras are still functional, though no longer relevant in the world of digital photography; the tape decks are obsolete. Fortunately, those ceramic elephants, the tacky trophies of Southeast Asia, are no longer with us.

Everything you bought at the BX in Da Nang was paid for in Military Payment Certificates (MPCs). In theory, U.S. dollars were prohibited in Vietnam; servicemen were paid not in dollars but in MPC. When you went to the officer's club, ate at the mess hall, or bought a new pair of boots, you paid in MPC. Then once you left Vietnam to go on R and R or return to the United States, your remaining MPC were fully convertible into dollars.

It was a bizarre-looking currency, made to order for a wartime economy. There were no coins, only colorful bank notes, ranging from five cents to twenty dollars. The bills were smaller than U.S. notes, were more cheaply made, and tended to wad up in your wallet or pocket.

The basic idea was that without U.S. dollars in circulation, the local South Vietnamese currency (the dong) would remain stable. Since it was illegal for unauthorized personnel to possess MPCs (so went the theory), the dong would be unchallenged. Not surprisingly, the local merchants refused to go along with the system. Everywhere in Vietnam, MPCs were a respected and well-used currency, surpassed in value only by the U.S. dollar.

The real danger to the local black market came when a new series of MPCs was issued and the old notes became worthless. Conversion day (or C-Day) was unannounced and was supposedly classified. Military personnel were restricted to base as they exchanged their old MPCs for the new series, while the nightclubs, prostitutes, and other entrepreneurs were left with worthless currency. Again, that was the theory; it rarely worked out that way, since the smart black marketers usually managed to get the early word and avoid being caught on C-Day with expired MPCs.

The MPC conversion only really affected me when I out-processed from Vietnam, and headed back to the U.S. The government had a savings bank for military personnel in Vietnam that paid a generous ten percent interest (about three or four percent better than most banks were paying at the time). I had managed to scrimp and save, accumulating nearly $10,000. A few days before I left, I went by the base bank (which was actually just a trailer) to pick up a check to take home, only to find out that my savings were in MPCs, not dollars. If I wanted the money, I had to take cold, hard cash. I stuffed the $10,000 in currency (I think it was all in $20 bills) in my pocket, enjoyed being flush with cash for a few minutes, then went next door and converted the sum to more sensible traveler's checks.

The 366th Dispensary, which is where I spent most of my days, was a series of interconnected modular buildings. There were three or four flight surgeons, as well as three or four general medical officers on the staff, each with an office in the main unit. Attached to the rear was a small hospital with about twenty-five beds. My office in the one story modular complex had a desk and examining table, but little else. The previous occupant had kindly left a poster on the back of the door to my office that read, "Today is the First Day of the Rest of Your Life." This seemed as good a way as any to look at my upcoming twelve months at Da Nang.

For the first several months of my tour, our hospital served as an aeromedical evacuation unit, an important link in the complex system of medical triage and evacuation. U.S. troops injured in combat were evacuated by helicopter to field hospitals. Since it was nearly impossible to move the wounded overland in Vietnam, these "dust off" choppers provided the critical first step in the process. If you could get an injured soldier to a medical facility alive, he had a 99% chance of surviving.

Once the wounded soldier was stabilized and the logistics were worked out, he would come to our unit at Da Nang for a few days before being flown out to hospitals in Japan, Okinawa, or the Philippines. Sick and injured patients were evacuated, as were any combat casualties. We saw a lot of accidents, as well as respiratory infections, hepatitis, and dysentery. There were a variety of ways to lose your life in Vietnam; more than ten thousand Americans died from non-combat causes.

Our hospital and our air evac unit were in the same wing and were staffed by the same nurses. I would make rounds twice a day, writing orders and doing the things you do for any sick or wounded patient. I always tried to strike a positive note and offer words of encouragement to every patient. It wasn't particularly difficult to do; no matter how bad the problem, everyone perked up when they were reminded that they were going home.

The aeromedical evacuation system itself was a complex form of triage. Some patients were priority, some were urgent, and some were routine; our job was to take care of them all. We had to make sure they were stable enough to handle the long flights.

The flight schedules were anything but regular. Bad weather, aircraft breakdowns, and problems at the receiving hospitals on the other end all created a lot of uncertainty. Often I'd have a room full of problem patients to worry about—the man with the persistent fever, the one with a drop in his hemoglobin level, the wounded soldier who had just learned that his wife had left him—and these concerns would gnaw at the back of my mind, worrying me at night and making it difficult to sleep. Then one afternoon I'd walk over from my office to make rounds, and the patients would be gone. I rarely got word, if there was word, of when the plane was coming to take them away. The aircraft would land, the flight nurses and other personnel would load them aboard the plane, and they were gone.

I tried to stay positive myself, as well. You knew that many of the sick and injured would fully recover; but they were the lucky ones. The less fortunate had lost limbs, suffered serious burns, or had other permanent problems. Sometimes it was difficult to keep from crying at their bedside, seeing the very young, injured in the prime of their life in a war without meaning.

At the height of the conflict, in 1968–1969, over a thousand casualties a month were being evacuated. Casualty Staging Flight facilities at places like Da Nang and Cam Ranh Bay had one hundred beds or more. Fortunately, by the time I arrived, it had slowed to a trickle; a dozen or less was the usual census in 1971.

By late fall of 1971, most of the American ground troops were gone. By that time, President Nixon's "Vietnamization" program had been underway for some time. The plan was to gradually turn the war over to the South Vietnamese, leaving some U.S. air power and advisors to keep things in check.

I was thankful that there would be no more battlefield casualties to look after and happy for the soldiers and Marines who no longer had to fight the brutal war. The air campaign continued unabated, but the war in the sky had a different dynamic, a different feel from the ground war. If you were shot down, you faced the quick death of combat, the hell of captivity, or the joy of being rescued. You were unlikely to end up in my hospital. Once the ground troops left, I was free to concentrate on the more traditional duties of a flight surgeon—taking care of the men who flew the airplanes.

For almost as long as there have been airplanes, there have been flight surgeons. The concept started back in World War I, continued in both war and in peace, and is an important component of today's Air Force. It's one of the best jobs in the USAF, a splendid opportunity to learn a lot about aerospace medicine and put your skills to direct use. I was fortunate to live and work with people who knew a great deal about flying and were happy to share their knowledge with me.

The Vietnam War was a boom time for the flight surgeon business. During the year I spent at Da Nang, there were more than seven hundred flight surgeons serving in the USAF. The majority were people like me: physicians who had finished medical school, completed a one-year internship, and were fulfilling a two-year military commitment. The Air Force appealed to doctors in a number of ways, but the biggest accommodation made to physicians was the requirement of only a two-year tour of active duty, instead of the usual four years.

More than a hundred doctors were in my class at flight surgeon school (more formally known as the Primary Course in Aerospace Medicine). Most of us had just finished a busy year of internships before coming to Brooks Air Force Base in San Antonio, Texas in early July. For an overworked intern, it was like arriving in heaven.

In flight surgeon's school, we only went to classes during the day, and there was no night call or weekend duty. For the first time in a long time I had the time and money to go to a movie or eat out at a restaurant.

During the two months at San Antonio, we studied aerospace physiology and pathology, public health, preventive medicine, and other interesting fields that rarely come up during an internship. Many of the instructors were career flight surgeons who had completed a three-year residency in aerospace medicine as well as a tour in Southeast Asia.

We all had a lot of exposure to aviation in our course at Brooks AFB; things like altitude chambers and ejection seats, but we never flew. Flight surgeons aren't pilots. The whole experience of flying was new to me. When I first signed on with the USAF a couple of years before graduating from medical school, I had never even flown in an airplane before. In the 1960s, flying was a quick, efficient way of traveling for the relatively affluent public; it had little of the "cattle car" ambiance of today's commercial aviation.

But in wartime, things can (sometimes) happen quickly, if you let them. In just a few brief years, I went from wondering what it was like to fly in an airplane to being an active crewmember in the backseat of a Mach-2 fighter in combat. I knew I was lucky, but I sometimes wondered if I had stepped too quickly or aimed too high.

Much of the enjoyment I took from flying came from being around the people who flew the planes. Pilots and WSOs are intelligent, practical, well-motivated individuals who are action oriented and able to handle stress efficiently. Fighter pilots love to fly, and they are very good at it. Normally, flying is built on routines, but in combat, it's an adventure as well as a job. The men in my squadron were aggressive and competitive, but good team players at the same time, emotionally stable and able to make snap judgment calls. Some of the older pilots had attended the Naval Academy, while many of the younger ones were Air Force Academy graduates. By and large, they had degrees in fields like business and engineering; philosophy or sociology majors were rare. Plus, service academy graduates have that strong sense of duty and a love of country that is often missing from many college graduates.

Often, the physicians who chose to become flight surgeons tended to emulate, or at least admire, many of these personality traits. Speaking personally, I liked and respected fighter pilots; we had a mutual admiration. They had a high regard for my medical education and for the fact that I had volunteered to live and fly with them. I knew that they flew the top fighters in the world in combat and I was excited that they were going to take me along for the ride.

FOUR

INTO THE SKY

June 26, 1971

IT TOOK ME a good six weeks from arrival in country to make it into the air. There was no book or schedule that set out the rules and procedures for a flight surgeon flying combat missions in an F-4 Phantom. I had to beg, plead, and scheme to get off the ground; it never would have happened on its own.

The basic reason it took so long was simple. My unit, the 390th Tactical Fighter Squadron, didn't really need me. The backseat of an F-4 was normally occupied by a Weapons System Officer (WSO) who had spent years acquiring the needed skills. I was an unnecessary appendage; someone who could contribute a warm body and little else to a combat mission.

In my view, fighter pilots were young, heroic, almost romanticized figures. They were a breed apart from the rest of the Air Force—flying dangerous missions, taking anti-aircraft fire, missiles, and MiGs, and never once complaining. I admired them greatly and was anxious to be a part of the squadron. Fortunately, they respected me as a physician; but more importantly, the 390th was proud that I had volunteered to be their flight surgeon. (During my year at Da Nang, neither of the other two F-4 squadrons had a flight surgeon.)

On paper, my orders to Vietnam had assigned me to the 366th Dispensary. My main duty was to provide medical care to the Air Force personnel at Da Nang Air Base, with a special emphasis on the pilots, navigators, and other crew members who flew the aircraft.

What did that entail? When most of the pilots and navigators first arrived on base, they would drop their medical records by the dispensary. These medical records were supposed to be hand-carried from one assignment to the next by the individual, but this was a fragile system; documents would get lost or disappear in the bureaucratic maze of the military. It was my job to make sure they had the correct paperwork, including an Air Force Form 137. This form was a set of footprints taken with ink, much the same as you would record someone's fingerprints. These footprints were a solemn reminder of the dangers inherent in flying; after a fire or crash, a foot encased in a boot was often the only way of positively identifying a victim.

In addition, all of the aircrew members had detailed physicals at least once a year, with no exceptions made for wartime. When the pilots were sick, I took them off flying status. They were grounded, assigned to DNIF (Duty Not Involving Flying.) When they were healthy, I cleared them once again to fly.

In most cases the decision was clear cut, but there were a few gray areas. In general, pilots in a fighter squadron want to fly; this is the principal reason they're in the Air Force. Even in wartime, they are anxious to return to the sky. I felt that if I got to know the men as individuals, I could make better calls.

A month or so before I arrived at Da Nang, I'd received a letter from one of the flight surgeons who would be rotating home around the same time that I would be arriving. He laid out the choices: I could stay in the medical hootch with the general medical officers, a few other flight surgeons, some dentists and a couple of medical administrators, or I could choose to live with any of the squadrons on base.

Flight surgeons are rated officers, meaning that they participate in "regular and frequent flights." Like pilots, navigators, and a few others, they are entitled to wear wings and also receive additional pay and benefits. So flight surgeons are on flying status, but they only need twelve hours or so of flying time each quarter to qualify for flight pay. An occasional trip on a transport plane flying from one base to another base would easily fulfill that requirement. If you wished, you could tag along on a flight from Da Nang to Saigon; the pilot would list you on the manifest, and you could sit in the back of the aircraft and read a book while earning flying time. In other words, a flight surgeon was primarily a physician, he could make as much or as little of flying as he desired.

For me, it was an easy choice—the chance to fly an F-4 Phantom in combat was too good an opportunity to pass up. It fueled a sense of adventure, answered the need for a challenge. This was the real thing; it wasn't an incidental, meaningless activity that I could do in my spare time. I would have to work hard to learn my job. So, unlike most everyone else in the squadron, I ended up being assigned to an F-4 squadron by choice. Every one of my fifty-plus combat missions was flown as a volunteer.

People mature at different ages. I was young and well educated, but not very wise for a man with a wife and son. I didn't choose to go to Vietnam, but since I was there, I wanted some tangible sense of accomplishment; something I could look back on with pride.

I had grown up in the 1950s in rural Mississippi, a state that still celebrates Robert E. Lee's birthday. My first eight years of education were spent at a small Catholic elementary school taught by an order of nuns from Kentucky. This was at the height of the Cold War, and there was no greater enemy of freedom and faith than communism. We were certain that our cause was just, and we knew that "those godless communists" were ineligible for the afterlife. The courage and moral rectitude of the Christian martyrs were held up as noble goals worth pursuing. There was no higher virtue for a young man to strive for than valor.

Many of us learn these things growing up; or, at least, we used to. And while you never completely bought in, those ideals provided a framework for your actions, a sort of default setting.

I knew that there was no greater litmus test for courage than flying fighters in combat, but at the same time, I've always been a realist. I knew I wasn't ready to become John Wayne, but I figured that if I could slip in through the back door and get close enough to combat, maybe a little of the bravery of fighter pilots might rub off on me.

I was very aware that few people would ever have this opportunity—flying in a Mach 2 fighter, watching anti-aircraft fire streak through the sky and explode into white puffs as you rolled in on a target. The excitement and challenge of flying in combat were there for the taking—I just had to reach out and take it.

I also looked forward to the friendship and camaraderie. A fighter squadron lives through good times and bad times as a unit; it's both a communal and a personal experience. Nobody lives small; it's a rich, full life, and I knew I would be foolish to pass up the chance.

Not to mention, I loved everything about the Phantom. I loved the speed, the sound, the smell. At Da Nang, even after flying dozens of missions, I still enjoyed lying in bed at night and listening to the roar of a flight of F-4s taking off, heading to work in the darkness of night over the Ho Chi Minh Trail. My barracks were only a quarter mile or so from the flight line, and I could feel the walls vibrate as the planes thundered into the air.

Much of my interest in fighters came from my first assignment at Hurlburt Field in Florida with an A-37 Dragonfly squadron. Originally a trainer, the Dragonfly was a twin engine aircraft with side-by-side seating. The controls were identical on both sides and it was a perfect see one, do one situation for a beginner like me. I could watch everything the pilot did and attempt to replicate his actions.

Compared to a Phantom, the A-37 was small and slow, a bit like comparing a budget car to a Formula One racer. The Dragonfly sat waist high off the ground; at times, it had the look of a plane you'd see at an amusement park. To get into the cockpit of an F-4, you had to scale a ladder some 15 feet in the air; for an A-37, you simply threw a leg over the side and swung in like you were climbing into a convertible.

That said, the Dragonfly was no toy; it was a tough aircraft that could carry its own weight in both fuel and armament. The plane was good value, too; you could buy a half dozen A-37s for the cost of one Phantom. The Dragonfly was slower over the target but more accurate than the fast movers. Most of its missions were in the southern part of South Vietnam in close air support of ground troops. It never went north like the F-105 and F-4s, but many South Vietnamese and American soldiers owe their life to the A-37.

Personally, I owe my air legs to the A-37. The worst thing that can happen to a flight surgeon, or anyone in pilot training, is to get airsick. I was lucky; I never had that problem, and by the time I got to Da Nang I was totally comfortable in an airplane.

At Hurlburt, we flew regular missions at the bombing range at Eglin AFB. The range was laid out like a bull's eye, with an observer stationed in a nearby tower to record your accuracy. The dummy bombs would create a small puff of white smoke as they struck the ground, hopefully in the center of the bull's-eye. The missions to the bombing range were a lot slower, were flown at a lower altitude, and were more controlled than real combat in Vietnam, but the basics were similar. My body soon got accustomed to the rigors of dive bombing.

The best days in an A-37 were those spent at the acrobatics range. We'd practice loops, barrel rolls, Immelmanns, and other acrobatic tricks. The pilot would do a maneuver, then I would try it. It was like teaching your thirteen-year-old son to drive a car.

By the time I had been at Da Nang for a couple of weeks, I had met most of the people in my squadron. They knew my name, or at least knew I was the squadron flight surgeon. Since wars are usually fought by the young, most of the guys were in their twenties and thirties.

I didn't know a whole lot about the flight schedule, but I gradually learned how things worked, mainly from watching and listening. The squadron had a scheduling officer who would usually receive the orders for the next day's missions in the late afternoon. These orders were called the "frag" (an abbreviation for "fragmentary order"). Each unit received only a portion, or fragment, of the daily strike plan. He would post the following day's schedule around six o'clock in the evening. It was all on a large Plexiglas board behind the scheduling desk, the flight call sign, crew members, and take off time written in grease pencil.

I would drop by the desk from time to time, acting like I was looking for my name on the schedule, and casually mention that I was ready to fly. The scheduling officer had a hundred and one things to keep up with, but he said he would check it out and see what he could do. This was wartime, after all; there were a lot bigger problems to deal with than getting me into the air.

The real problem was that the 390th had been at Da Nang for years but hadn't always had a flight surgeon. My predecessor did an outstanding job, but I was the new kid on the block. If you were a pilot or WSO, you followed a well-laid out plan for getting checked out for combat, but no one knew how things worked for a flight surgeon. Flight surgeons had flown in the backseat of Phantoms since the beginning of the Vietnam War, but it was a hit-and-miss situation.

It wasn't a simple task finding out what was allowed by regulation (the Air Force, like the rest of the military, lives and dies by regulations). On the wall opposite the scheduling desk was a bookshelf filled with large volumes—USAF regulations, PACAF (Pacific Air Force) regulations, Seventh Air Force regulations. These books, by and large, sat gathering dust. The scheduling officer leafed through some of the books, looking for guidance on my flying status. What kinds of missions could I fly? Where was I permitted to go? How often could I fly? He might as well have been searching the IRS tax code for directions; he wanted to help me, but he couldn't really tell me where I stood.

I felt a little embarrassed. I'm sure in the squadron's eyes, my question was a minor one. The ground war was winding down, but the air war was still running wide open. The squadron had more serious problems to attend to than accommodating a novice flight surgeon. I felt like I was waiting on a light that might never turn green.

So I decided to lend a hand and search through the regulations myself, hoping to speed the process along. A day or so later, in the Seventh Air Force regulations, I found the applicable rule for flight surgeons flying in combat. I don't remember the exact wording, but the rules were restrictive and confusing, with a very long list of what you couldn't do. A flight surgeon seemed to be allowed to fly in just a few circumstances, mostly non-combat.

Now, the Seventh Air Force regulations were kept in a three-ring, loose leaf binder, so the rules could easily be updated as new edicts came down. I shuffled around, thumbing through pages, trying my best to look like a scholar of military regulations. Then, when no one was watching, I removed the pages pertaining to flight surgeons, stuck them in my pocket, and went about my business.

The talk about rules and regulations gradually faded away.

Decades later, I found out some of the reasons for the uncertainty over flight surgeons flying combat missions in an F-4 in Vietnam. Part of it had to do with the Phantom itself; it's a two-seat aircraft with dual controls. The backseater (originally a pilot in the early years of the war, and later a navigator) had essential tasks to perform in regards to navigation, weapons delivery, and communication. This was an airplane where the second man wasn't "along for the ride"—he was an active, essential crew member. The job couldn't be faked. It was one thing to take a flight surgeon along on a trip to the bombing range in an A-37, but it was something else entirely to place him in the backseat of an F-4 in combat.

An even bigger reason for limiting a flight surgeon's role in combat came in 1966, when a flight surgeon in the backseat of an F-4 was lost in combat. The order came down from the Seventh Air Force that no flight surgeon could fly in combat; in some ways, the Air Force seemed to value flight surgeons more highly than fighter pilots. Someone pointed out that flight surgeons were on flying status and had to fly, so the rules were modified: flight surgeons could fly maybe twice a month, and then maybe once a week, then maybe just on certain missions, and only if the wing commander approved.

In other words, nobody really knew, and if anybody did know, they probably didn't care; it was whatever you could get away with. I knew nothing at all of this at the time. I only knew that I needed a little help getting into the air.

A few days later, I went to see my squadron commander, Lt. Colonel Jacobs. He was our father figure, the well-respected leader of our squadron, and the closest thing we had to God at Da Nang. I was honored that he made time to see me.

I told Colonel Jacobs that it was important to me to fly in an F-4, stressing that it was part of my duties as a flight surgeon, almost implying that the USAF was negligent for not putting me in the air. I pointed out that I was married with a young family and I needed the flight pay (omitting the fact that I could have easily qualified without flying in a Phantom).

Colonel Jacobs was busy, and probably didn't have time to figure out how to say no. He told me he'd check on it, and we left it at that. The next day, I got a note in my box to see Captain Jack, one of the squadron instructor pilots (IP).

I was on my way.

Early on in the Vietnam War, the Air Force adopted a one-tour policy. If you had spent a year in Southeast Asia, you didn't have to go back for a second tour until everyone else had gone. The idea was to spread the risks—as well as the career advantages—of combat to everyone in the Air Force. After all, if you hoped to advance in the military, you had to punch your ticket in a combat assignment.

At the beginning of the war, fighter pilots usually went into combat after flying fighters elsewhere. As they rotated home, replacement training units in the U.S. sent over new pilots fresh out of pilot training, as well as others who were cross-trained into fighters from previous assignments with bombers and transports. (The Navy, by contrast, tended to keep their fighter squadrons more intact and deployed them on cruises multiple times.)

Some have criticized this policy, claiming that only a certain type of pilot has the skills and temperament needed to become a successful fighter pilot. Since I wasn't a pilot, I have no right to weigh in on the subject, but I quickly became aware that some pilots and WSOs were better than others. Everyone in the squadron knew who the good sticks were; no one had to give me a list, I quickly found out. The great thing was that since I was the lowest common denominator in the squadron, I always got paired with the top pilots, the flight leaders.

Let me go into a bit more detail on the F-4 Phantom itself. The Phantom is a two-seat aircraft, with the pilot in the front seat and the backseater directly behind and slightly above him. Originally, the man in the back was also a pilot, but a year or so before I came to Vietnam the Air Force began eliminating backseat pilots and started assigning navigators to that spot. Unlike the F-4s flown by the Navy, the back cockpit of an Air Force F-4 has a stick, rudder pedals, and throttles; this allows the backseater to fly the plane as needed.

The front seat pilot was the Aircraft Commander who did all the serious work (though if the mission went well, the backseater would often get a chance to fly the plane back to base). The official title of the backseater, Weapon Systems Officer (WSO), was rarely used at Da Nang; the man in the rear was simply known as the GIB (Guy in the Back) or backseater. So, if you wanted to ask a pilot who he flew with, you would say, "Who was your backseater?" or "Who was your GIB?"

Captain Jack looked like a fighter pilot sent straight from central casting: six feet tall, blond, and built like a linebacker. He had that quiet cool that inspires trust. Like all IPs, he was one of the best pilots in the squadron. (It's the one job in the Air Force that seems to be based totally on ability rather than on rank. Our squadron had first lieutenants in their initial assignment who became IPs near the end of their tour. It was a true meritocracy.)

Jack had a charisma and drive that made you listen closely to what he said. He talked as if he had confidence in me. Jack told me what to do and I did it. Without trying, he had me ready to follow orders, to march to the sound of the cannon. He told me that flying fighters was a serious, dangerous business; we took no unnecessary risks because the necessary risks were bad enough. He didn't smile; this was no punch line, it was the simple truth.

Jack laid out a plan and told me what he expected from me. I started with the basics, things like the byzantine rules of engagement, a list of limitations that seemed designed to victimize fighter pilots. I memorized the emergency procedures, or tried to; everyone carried a yellow set of emergency procedures for the F-4 that you had to be able to recite in your sleep. These were stored in a small canvas bag that you carried with you in the cockpit, known as the ditty bag or doofer bag. The bag also contained your checklists and gloves, as well as the maps you needed to help navigate. There were four or five maps that, combined, covered most of the areas where you would be flying, mainly the Laotian panhandle and the I Corps region of South Vietnam.

I sat in on a couple of mission briefings and debriefings, paying particular attention to what the backseaters did and said. Sometimes the flight leader planned on delivering the bombs manually, other times, dive toss was chosen. Dive toss was a weapons release computer system that required the GIB to get a radar lock as the aircraft rolled in on a target. If the backseater failed to get the lock, the ordnance wasn't released.

Heading over to the life support shack, I met with Sergeant Joe, a man I knew was an important element in staying alive. The first thing Joe did was take the flight helmet that I'd brought with me from Florida and change the color from a bright white to a camouflage. The Phantoms were all painted in camouflage, and I had no wish for my head to serve as a bull's eye for some enemy gunner.

I was also fitted with a G-suit, a snug, form-fitting device worn over the flight suit that covered me from the waist down to the ankles. The G-suit, more accurately known as the anti-G suit, could double in a pinch as a hernia truss: it had air bladders over the abdomen, thighs, and calves. A hose about eighteen inches long hung from the left waist area, looking like someone had sewn a piece of garden hose onto the waist band. Once you were strapped into the cockpit, you plugged the hose into an outlet that sensed the amount of G forces. Normally, we experience one G (or one gravity force) in everyday life. During combat maneuvers in an F-4, it's common to experience five or even six times as much force, known as "pulling" 5 or 6 G's. As the G's increase, the bladders in the G-suit inflate, counteracting the forces acting on the body. Without a G-suit, high G forces can push the blood from the brain and upper body into the lower body, resulting in a temporary blackout or even total loss of consciousness. Tunnel vision, one of the first signs of high G forces, was very common when pulling out of a steep dive. The peripheral vision would gradually narrow as the G forces increased; when the forces diminished, your full visual field would return.

My G-suit also served other functions; there was room for a knife that fit snugly along the inner thigh and was attached to a long piece of cord, and the lower part of each leg had room for a water flask. I also got fitted with a survival vest and parachute harness. The vest carried two radios, a couple of smoke flares, a compass, a first aid kit, and several other useful items, including enough extra rounds of .38 caliber ammunition for a long gun battle. Although the survival vest was made of lightweight nylon material, by the time I added the parachute harness and strapped on a Smith & Wesson .38 caliber revolver, I weighed a good forty pounds more than when I started.

I had already been listening carefully to what Sergeant Joe was telling me as we covered the G-suit and survival vest, but when we got to the next topic, I started paying *very* close attention, focusing completely on his instructions.

Joe began explaining the ejection seat of an F-4—i.e., the link between surviving and dying. One of the GIB's responsibilities was to do a pre-flight check of the front and back ejection seats. When

I flew in the A-37s in Florida, I never gave a second thought to ejecting from an aircraft. Here at Da Nang, it became a major concern, almost an obsession.

Thankfully, the F-4 Phantom was blessed with Martin-Baker MK-H7 ejection seats. Many of the older ejection seats required the aircraft to attain a certain speed and certain altitude in order for the crew to survive. If you were too close to the ground, you were out of luck; your parachute wouldn't have time to deploy. The Martin-Baker ejection seat, by contrast, had a zero-zero capability (referring to zero velocity, zero altitude). You could be sitting on the runway, eject, and still survive. Once the frontseater or backseater activates the system, they're both shot into the air in less than a second and a half. The rear canopy blows first and the backseater is shot out of the rear cockpit in around .54 seconds; the front canopy then blows and the pilot is up and away approximately 1.39 seconds after initiation. (This was the theory, anyway. A few of the guys had stories where things didn't quite work out in a zero-zero setting.)

It might not have been perfect, but a lot of F-4 pilots and backseaters have Martin-Baker to thank for their lives. A small family-owned British company that still operates today, Martin-Baker counts well over seven thousand successful ejections since 1949. They still dominate the ejection seat business, but the peak of their fifty-plus years of manufacturing ejection seats came from F-4s during the Vietnam War.

I didn't need to be sold on the product. Sergeant Joe gave me a list of things to check on the ejection seats before flying—switches, safety pins, cables, etc.—and I learned them as if my life depended on it.

I was feeling pretty good. I was learning a lot about Phantoms, and felt I knew a fair amount from having flown A-37s in Florida. (In reality, I just didn't know enough to know how *little* I knew.)

My roommate was a WSO, and he helped me a lot by explaining procedures, telling me problems to avoid, and answering all my questions. Most importantly, the fact that I was going to fly F-4s now seemed to be a given. It was now a question of when, not if.

Jack called me at the dispensary one morning and told me, "Doc, I've got a plane. Meet me at 2:00 PM at the squadron briefing room." I was getting the non-credit introductory course in flying the F-4. I was excited; I felt like a minor league baseball player who had gotten a call to the majors.

I had been out to the flight line several times, introducing myself and working with the crew chiefs, so I knew where to go. The Phantoms were parked under concrete revetments, protected from rocket attacks.

It was love, awe, and fear at first sight. The shark-like nose gave the F-4s an angry, menacing look. The planes were some sixty feet long and dressed in war paint, the top a brown and green camouflage while the belly was white. The shark's mouth on the nose was bright red in color and studded with white teeth. There was a huge air intake on each side of the two main cockpits. The wings tilted up at the ends, while the horizontal stabilators in the rear pointed down. This was a plane with a lot of angles.

A good sixteen feet high, I had to climb a six-rung ladder temporarily mounted on the left of the front cockpit before I could slide into the back seat. The rear cockpit was sometimes called the "pit," and it gave you the feeling of being partway down a hole with limited visibility. The canopy rails on each side were high. The control stick was in the center, the rudder pedals were on the floor, and a pair of throttles was on the left. The backseat dashboard was filled with gauges, knobs, switches, dials, levers, and handles. The ejection seat was in the rear. This was no basic model aircraft. It was like whoever designed this plane had decided to spring for all the available options.

Our flight was a single-ship training mission; the F-4 would carry no ordnance. We didn't go to wing headquarters for an intelligence or weather briefing, we just picked up our gear at life support and headed to the aircraft.

Jack ran me through his pre-flight check and went through the routines. My pre-flights included the ejection seats and ordnance. I plugged in every tube and wire I could find—oxygen, radio, G suit. The crew chief made sure I was squared away, and we were soon ready. The command post cleared us to Da Nang ground and we taxied out, skipped the arming area before finally getting clearance for takeoff.

That was it; we were up and away, out over the South China Sea.

Jack covered a few basic emergencies, like unusual altitude recoveries, target fixation, and other problems. Next, we climbed up to around thirty-five thousand feet, pushed it into afterburners, and went supersonic. Since there aren't any available landmarks high in the sky—no land, no clouds, nothing to relate to—flying faster than the speed of sound wasn't much of a sensation. That was, until Jack came out of afterburners, and the deceleration felt as if a telephone pole was pushing me in the back toward the instrument panel.

Jack gave me the controls for a little bit. The throttles are for fast and slow, the stick is for right and left, up and down, and the trim button smoothes everything out, all of which makes it sound much simpler than it really is. I had a death grip on the stick, pushing the throttles like I owned the plane.

We headed home to Da Nang. It was a smooth landing, the drag chute deployed, and we taxied back to the revetment. It was a simple training flight for Captain Jack; an exhibition game that didn't count, checking out a slow learner in a fast mover, and almost assuredly a low point of his combat tour.

For me, it was so much more than another day at the office. I tried not to appear too excited, but I couldn't help but hope there were bigger things to come.

HO CHI MINH TRAIL

FIVE

LIFE IN THE BACKSEAT

1971–1972

As FALL APPROACHED, my life at Da Nang took on a regular pattern. Our medical dispensary was open seven days a week, around the clock, but we were fortunate to have enough physicians that everyone enjoyed a decent amount of time off. Our group of flight surgeons worked well together, filling in when someone was off flying, helping each other with difficult cases, and sharing the challenges and rewards of practicing medicine in the military during wartime.

My DEROS calendar, initially a blank white page, began to take shape as I colored it in with each passing day. Simple things took on a special meaning; my greatest pleasure was the daily mail delivery. Letters and pictures from my family were my greatest treasure, a reminder of what was waiting when I returned from Vietnam.

New arrivals, many of whom had the same forlorn, bewildered look that I once had, showed up regularly. We celebrated—even as we envied—the old-timers as they rotated back home.

Even though I wished I was back home, things were better than when I first arrived. I had been in country just a few months, but I had learned where to go when I needed help, who to see, who to avoid, what to always do, and what to never even think about doing. I was becoming an old hand, even as my days were becoming routine.

Except when it came to flying.

I found out very early on that there was no such thing as a "routine" combat mission. Flying fighters was often full of surprises and loaded with challenges. Equipment on the plane sometimes didn't work like it was supposed to, the weather often failed to cooperate, and people on the ground shot at you. There were dozens of ways for things to go bad in wartime.

During the Vietnam War, an F-4 Phantom cost several million dollars. It was a sophisticated fighter with advanced radar, computers, engines, the works. The planes flew around the clock and were pushed to their limits by the pilots who flew them. The Phantom required multiple work hours of maintenance for every hour in the air, and it was almost impossible to keep everything working all of the time. Sometimes it was a navigational system, other times a problem with the radar.

The whole air war in Vietnam revolved around the weather. The I Corps region and the Laotian panhandle had opposite monsoon weather patterns. In the fall and early winter, it seemed to rain constantly at Da Nang, while in Laos on the other side of the Annamite Mountains it was the dry season, and traffic was heavy on the Ho Chi Minh Trail. If you caught a good weather pattern at Da Nang, you were usually out of luck over the Trail; only rarely did you have favorable weather at home and over the target.

The F-4 wasn't an all-weather fighter—things tended to work best when the pilot could actually see the target. There were ways of delivering ordnance in bad weather, but they weren't very accurate. Good weather was needed not only to see the target but, more importantly, to see the people on the ground shooting at you. It could be small arms fire, anti-aircraft artillery (AAA), or even surface-to-air missiles (SAMs) along the passes on the North Vietnamese border.

After a couple of additional training flights, I started flying regular combat missions. During the summer of 1971, the 390th flew some close air support sorties in support of American troops in the field, but by the fall, the last U.S. combat ground troops were gone from Vietnam. (American air power and military advisors weren't as fortunate, they remained until 1973.)

In the fall of 1968, Lyndon Johnson ended the Rolling Thunder bombing of North Vietnam, a campaign he began in early 1965. After Rolling Thunder, American strategy changed. No longer were we looking to destroy supplies headed to South Vietnam while they were still in North Vietnam. Instead, the materiel would be interdicted while moving on the Ho Chi Minh Trail in the Laotian panhandle.

Most of the combat missions I flew were over the Trail in the Laos panhandle, an area we knew as Steel Tiger. When I went to Da Nang initially, I wasn't familiar with the world "interdiction," but I would hear it constantly during my tour. The basic idea was to use armed forces to slow down or stop the flow of supplies and personnel needed by an enemy to continue hostilities. In other words, if you cut down on their food and ammunitions, they wouldn't be able to continue fighting.

In retrospect, it wasn't a great strategy. Instead of destroying the trucks and supplies while they were bunched together on a train from China or were begin unloaded at the port of Haiphong, the U.S. elected to wait until they were all spread out along the Trail and covered by a triple canopy jungle, making them difficult to locate and even harder to destroy.

Making matters worse, the North Vietnamese had begun improving the Ho Chi Minh Trail in 1959, and they'd never slowed down. By the time I arrived, twelve years later, they had developed a highly sophisticated network covering some twelve thousand miles, almost all of which was covered by a canopy of trees. There were underground oil pipelines, heavy road equipment, and thousands of permanent workers. Early in the war, porters carrying supplies on their back and men pushing loaded bicycles were used to move supplies; in some cases, elephants were pressed into service. By 1971, almost everything was moved by trucks, and these vehicles were our targets.

Most of the time, we worked with a Forward Air Controller (FAC) who flew in a lighter, slower aircraft at a lower altitude, looking for targets for the fighters to strike. The FAC often had a definite area of responsibility that he flew over regularly. Subtle changes in the terrain, unnoticed by most everyone else, would allow the FAC to detect suspicious activities.

Every sortie we flew was different, but there was a common pattern for all flights. Most of our missions were two-ship flights. The pilot of the lead aircraft, the flight leader, was responsible for planning, briefing, tactics, and all other aspects of the mission. His responsibility and authority were clear and distinct. I usually flew in the flight leader's back seat, since I was the least experienced and least knowledgeable person in the flight. The wingman was sometimes a newer pilot, and was usually paired with a senior GIB.

Our flight would meet around two hours before the scheduled takeoff at the mission planning room at wing headquarters. The 366th Tactical Flight Wing lived, worked, and flew out of the southeast corner of the base, so everything was within convenient walking distance. Before heading to mission planning, I would leave my wallet and all other personal items in my room; I'd even strip the wing insignia off my flight suit. The only identification I carried was my dog tags. I guess the idea was that if you ejected from an F-4 and were captured, the communists would have to guess who you were and where you came from.

The mission planning room had long rows of tables with large, thick folders perched on top. The folders contained target information, such as maps, photos, FAC call signs, radio frequencies, and other data. The room was usually crowded with pilots and WSOs from the three squadrons of the 366th, all preparing for their missions. There was no idle chit-chat; very little conversation at all, in fact. The mission was drawing nearer, and everyone was concentrating on the task ahead. This was usually when we would learn exactly where we were going and precisely what target we were scheduled to hit. I would thumb through the target folder, look at the pictures, double check my maps, and write down any information I thought we might need.

I noticed one common trait of fighter pilots during my year at Da Nang; sort of an unwritten, unspoken rule. No one ever complained before a mission about where they were being sent. Everyone knew what was involved; it was understood that you flew where you were supposed to fly and you did your job, regardless of the target location. After the mission, you could bitch and moan, curse and complain to your heart's content, but you never did so before the flight.

To give an example, I was never happy when I looked up the coordinates in mission planning and found out we were headed to the Mu Gia Pass area. Mu Gia was the main entry point from North Vietnam onto the Ho Chi Minh Trail. The North Vietnamese side of the pass had large caliber AAA as well as SAM sites. Mu Gia Pass wasn't the real North Vietnam, like the men of Rolling Thunder experienced, but it was in the neighborhood, close enough for a frightened flight surgeon. My fear and anxiety levels would increase a couple of notches and my stomach would feel a little queasy, but I kept my mouth shut because the people around me did the same.

After we gathered our target info, we headed to the adjacent briefing room for a weather update. The room had a dais with a podium and several large maps covering the back wall. There were probably twenty or so folding chairs lined in semicircular rows facing the maps. The weatherman spoke for ten minutes or so, telling us the expected weather for takeoff, en route, over the target, and on landing. It was hard, straightforward, useful data, with none of the contrived enthusiasm that seems to be a part of the genetic makeup of today's weatherman. The weather was very important; heavy clouds and low ceilings made everything that much riskier. As the weather went, so often went the mission.

The intelligence briefing followed the weather briefing. We heard a few words about the war in general, sort of a big picture glimpse, but mostly we focused on what had been going on in the areas where our wing flew. The intel officer would describe what areas were getting AAA. Usually, he would name names: "Jones and Smith from the 4th got heavy flak at Ban Karai for the third day in a row," or, "Johnson and Roberts reported AAA near the catcher's mitt this morning." There was never a day off; someone was always getting shot at somewhere. The very worst news came when he reported that a plane had been shot down and the crew hadn't been rescued.

By the time the intel briefing was over, I was usually beginning to question my judgment, wondering what the hell I was doing in a place where so many bad things could happen. My bowels shaky, my nerves on edge, and my hopes for a jolt of courage unanswered, at that stage I wouldn't have been at all disappointed to have some mechanical problem with the plane and have to abort the mission.

After the briefings at wing headquarters, the four crewmembers of our flight would walk a few doors down to our squadron briefing room. Our flight leader would go over the details of our mission, including headings, radio frequencies, dive angles, number of passes, and direction to head if we were hit. He'd quiz us on emergency procedures; those were in a yellow loose ring notebook, and you were supposed to have them memorized. Finally, we'd get a time hack so that everyone was on an exact schedule.

After a final trip to the bathroom, the life support trailer was next. I'd put on my G-suit, survival vest, and parachute harness. I'd grab a couple of flasks of cool water from the refrigerator and store them in the bottom part of my G-suit. Everyone carried two radios; I always double-checked the charge and stuck an extra battery in my vest. Finally, I checked out and loaded a .38 revolver.

After life support, we walked to the flight line to pre-flight our aircraft. Since I was carrying an extra forty pounds of gear and the temperature was often over one hundred degrees, I was generally soaked with sweat by this time and was anxious to get in the air. These moments before takeoff were a time of great apprehension and anticipation for everyone. We had briefed the mission, but every mission was different, a story waiting to be written. No one knew what was going to unfold over the next few hours.

The flight line was a different world. The camouflaged, shark-toothed Phantom, fully-loaded; the smell of exhaust and jet fuel permeating the air; the deafening noise of jet aircraft coming and going in a confined area; the crew chiefs hustling about, often stripped to the waist. The heat, noise, vibration, activity, and anticipation made the tension almost palpable.

My responsibilities were to pre-flight the ejection seats and the ordnance. I would run through the check of the front and back seats at least twice. I had developed some kind of preoccupation, almost a compulsion, with the ejection seat. Certain pins belonged at certain places and were removed at certain times. If everything didn't check exactly, I called the crew at life support and had them come over and take a look.

Checking the ordnance was a simpler task; it would have been hard for me to foul things up. The bombs were off-loaded from a trolley onto the ejection racks by the munitions crew long before we arrived. Depending on the mission, we carried different types of weapons. A standard load was twelve MK-82 500-pound bombs, called "slicks" or "dumb bombs" (in contrast to the laser-guided "smart" bombs that came later in my tour). The bombs were long, green, and very menacing. The fusing of the bomb varied depending on the target. I'd push a little on each one to make sure it was secure on the ejector rack, and I'd also check to confirm the arming pin hadn't been pulled. No one wanted a bomb hot until just before takeoff.

As for the rest of our armaments, we normally carried radar-guided Sparrow missiles tucked up under the fuselage, though on some missions heat-seeking Sidewinders were added. Both of these missiles were designed to be used in aerial combat. The F-4 E models also had a 20 mm nose gun that the F-4 D version lacked. Other additions could include an Electronic Counter Measures (ECM) pod and a six hundred gallon centerline fuel tank. It got to where the underside of a loaded Phantom sometimes looked like an over-decorated Christmas tree.

I always made a point to talk to the crew chief during pre-flight; he knew the plane a lot better than I did. "Are there any problems; is there anything I need to know?" I let him know that I wanted to learn from him, that I was proud to be flying in his airplane. These men performed the unheralded but indispensable tasks that kept the Phantoms in the air.

Next, I would climb up the yellow ladder and slip into the rear cockpit. I would hook up my G-suit, connect the oxygen, attach my harness to the ejection seat, and connect the radio. I felt like I was cutting my link to the earth, attaching myself to a rocket bound for outer space. For the first few minutes, I'd perform a series of built-in tests, making sure the navigation, radar, and weapons systems were working properly.

At the pre-arranged time, usually seven minutes or so before scheduled take-off, our flight would contact the command post at wing headquarters to let them know we were on schedule and had the current weather.

"Blue Bird, Gunfighter 42, dash 2."

The command post would clear us to Da Nang Ground Control.

"Da Nang Ground, Gunfighter 42, taxi two Fox fours."

Da Nang Ground would give us runway instruction, and we were ready to roll. The crew chief would snap to attention and salute, the pilot would return the salute, and we'd taxi out of the revetment, with the wingman following maybe a hundred yards behind the leader.

A quick stop at the arming pit allowed the arming crew to give the aircraft a final check. The arming pins were pulled from the ordnance and held aloft to show the Aircraft Commander. The leader of the arming crew would salute and give a thumbs-up, and we'd be cleared onto the runway for take-off.

Both aircraft would line up, then the Aircraft Commander of the lead plane would run up each engine to 85 percent of full military power (full engine thrust without the afterburners) before bringing it back to idle, one engine at a time. Both engines were then pushed to full military power and the brakes released.

The ground shook, the engines roared; the race was on. Down the runway the Phantom rolled, and when the pilot lit the afterburners, the aircraft seemed to jump, as if it had finally slipped its leash. Some four thousand feet down the runway, at around 170 miles per hour or so, the nose wheel would life off. The stick was held back and, at around 200 miles per hour, the aircraft was off the ground.

After takeoff we'd usually roll left and head toward the South China Sea. I'd look down at the fading buildings and countryside as we climbed quickly. Nothing was ever totally safe at Da Nang; there had been a few instances of ground fire directed at planes taking off and landing, so the idea was not to linger very long.

The second aircraft in the flight would roll thirty seconds after the first, after which the lead would ease back on the power and the second plane would fly a cutoff angle to rejoin. Each aircraft would make a brief inspection of the other plane to make sure there were no problems on takeoff.

Shortly after takeoff we'd contact Panama, Da Nang's tactical radar control center located atop the nearby Monkey Mountain. Panama would vector us out of the area before turning us over to Hillsboro, the Airborne Battlefield Command and Control Center (ABCCC). Hillsboro, an airborne EC-130, ran the war in real time. Most of the time, our flight would head toward our scheduled rendezvous with the FAC, but occasionally we'd get airborne, contact Hillsboro, and find out that our target had changed. Hillsboro would give us the name and frequency of a new FAC to contact. Other times, during mission planning we'd have no information on a target whatsoever; simply instructions to contact Hillsboro once we were in the air.

Once our FAC had been confirmed, we'd change to another radio frequency to talk to the FAC (called "going tactical"). By this time we were often just fifteen minutes or so from the target. We'd tell the FAC who we were, what we were carrying, and how long we could spend over the target.

The FAC would give us a target brief, describing the target. Often it was a truck park, a POL (Petroleum, Oil, Lubricants) depot, a weapons cache, or a newly constructed road that needed to be cut. He would describe the location of any friendly forces (which were very rare over the Trail) or any bad guys (enemy troops, both

Viet Cong and North Vietnamese regulars, were appropriately known as "bad guys.") We'd get direction for run in, target altitude, and best escape route if hit. Most importantly, we'd get the FAC's location. Once we spotted him, he'd rock his wings for visual confirmation.

Our flight would circle the target in a counter clockwise wheel pattern, with the two F4s at roughly opposite sides of the wheel holding around 12,000 feet. That's high in the sky. The jungle from that altitude has a monotonous gray-green look, with just a few elevations and rivers for landmarks. There were no trails, no trucks, no sign of life. The targets have a sterile, featureless appearance from that altitude.

The FAC was flying much slower and a lot closer to the ground than we were. I would watch as he rolled inverted, pointed his nose toward the ground, and fired a Willie Pete (a white phosphorous rocket) before pulling out. A giant plume of smoke would gush out of the jungle canopy, easily visible from 12,000 feet, a solid point of reference on a bland green tableau.

"Gunfighter 42, place your bombs fifty meters east of my smoke."

There was a certain way of delivering ordnance during my year in Vietnam. I don't know if it was a written policy, a wing custom, a sacred formula, or what, but it rarely varied. The number of passes you made depended on your location. It was sort of a trouble pecking order, a hierarchy of danger. When we flew close air support, aiding troops in contact with the enemy, we normally made six passes, a couple of bombs at a time. The small arms fire you encountered in South Vietnam was less of a threat than the AAA you saw over the Trail. (In reality, when Americans or South Vietnamese troops were in danger, you flew at whatever altitude was required and made as many passes as necessary.)

Over the trail, we usually made three or four passes. In the more dangerous spots, like Mu Gia Pass along the North Vietnamese border, two passes were the custom. The pilots who flew over North Vietnam in Rolling Thunder and Linebacker followed, for good reason, the "one pass and haul ass" rule. North Vietnam was the most heavily defended area in the war; the risk there was many times greater than in Laos.

Of course, nobody ever asked my opinion on the number of passes required for any particular mission. The flight leader told us at our briefing the number of passes we were going to make and that was the way it would be done, unless the FAC had a very compelling reason to change it.

Once cleared by the FAC, the lead aircraft was first in.

"Gunfighter 42 is in hot, FAC in sight."

The FAC was usually holding off, well away from the target, but you had to be absolutely certain you knew his position.

Here's where things get interesting. The pilot would roll the Phantom left, nearly inverted, pointing the nose of the plane at a spot just beyond the target. When you're screaming toward the ground at a 45 degree angle, traveling over five hundred miles per hour, it feels like you're going straight down, like you've gone over a cliff; the ground seems to be getting very close very quickly. I would call out the numbers as the altimeter rapidly unwound. The AC would then roll the aircraft upright, wings level, and track the target for five to ten seconds before punching the pickle button on his stick. The release of the bombs made a little rumble, sort of like you've run over a speed bump in a car. It was a reassuring feeling; it meant that everything worked and no extra passes were needed. Normally, the bombs came off at around seven thousand feet and the aircraft bottomed out around four thousand feet.

The wings level tracking time that happened just prior to pickle was always a little disconcerting to me. It was like getting in line for a firing squad; things seem to move in slow motion, as you become the perfect target for anti-aircraft fire. The pilots liked to claim that they only got paid for five seconds of tracking time; anything longer was wasted.

Once the bombs were released, the AC pulled very hard, weaving, bobbing, and twisting (jinking) to avoid enemy fire. It was pickle, pull, roll, and jink. Sometimes I could catch a flash of an explosion by looking in the rearview mirrors, but you never heard the sound inside the cockpit.

Most of the time, our wing used a manual bomb delivery: the pilot would get the target in his sight, press the pickle button at the appropriate time, and the bombs would be released. The Phantom also had a weapons release computer system (WRCS) that, in theory, provided a more precise delivery. The main method we used was called dive toss.

During dive toss, the AC would roll in the same way as for manual delivery, placing his gunsight directly on the target. Meanwhile, in the backseat, a little blip would float down from the top of the radar screen and the GIB would have to manipulate the radar control handle, placing the cursor directly over the radar return and pressing a button to lock on. The computer would then read the altitude and dive angle and automatically release the bombs at the appropriate time. For the backseater, it was a real-life video game with real consequences; if you missed the lock, you had to make an extra pass, needlessly exposing yourself to ground fire.

In general, our wing preferred manual delivery over dive toss. I think part of it was the fighter pilot mentality. Most pilots felt they were trained to fly and fight, not to use a computer. This attitude got passed along as new crew members came on board.

Both aircraft in the flight would alternate making passes. After each pass, the FAC would make corrections and remark the target if necessary. Once we had exhausted our ordnance, the FAC would give us a bomb damage assessment (BDA). It was sort of like getting a report card, and it usually went something like this: "Two trucks destroyed," or, "One hundred meters of road cut," or, "80 percent of bombs within one hundred meters of target." I'd write down the BDA and repeat it; the FAC would thank us for a good job, and we'd compliment his work. Each aircraft would inspect the other plane for any damage from ground fire, and we'd join up in formation for the flight back to Da Nang.

Heading home, the backseaters often got to fly the plane. Throttles in the left hand, stick in the right hand, with the trim button to smooth things out, time went by fast at 400 miles per hour. Sometimes the wingman would lead and I would get to practice flying on his wing. I would try to do just as I was told, line up the light on the lead's wing with the star on his fuselage for proper formation alignment and ignore everything else. It was like a lot of things in flying, routine and simple—if you knew what you were doing. It was much more difficult for a novice like me.

Da Nang control would bring us in one ship at a time with no pitchout. We'd jettison the drag chute, taxi back to the revetment, and park the aircraft. The crew chief would unhook us and ask about the flight. "Any AAA?" they'd ask. "Any problems with the plane?" The crew would take a quick look for any damage from small arms fire. If I told them about something that didn't work in the backseat, the usual response was, "Damn Doc, you broke my airplane."

We'd drop our gear at life support and stop by maintenance debrief to fill out paperwork and tell them about any problems we'd had with the plane. It was just like taking your car to a repair shop. A sergeant would write out a repair order, and the next time you flew the aircraft the problem was (usually) fixed. Finally came a detailed intelligence debrief on the mission followed by a walk back to squadron headquarters, and it was over.

It was only around a five hour work day, in most instances, but it was always money well-earned.

SIX

PARTY SUITS

1971–1972

ABOUT ONCE A month, our squadron had a party. I've forgotten a lot about my year in Vietnam—in fact, I've forgotten quite a bit about my life in general—but the memories of those squadron parties are still vivid and clear. They were great celebrations; extended bouts of drinking, roasting, and storytelling, a sacred part of the combat fighter squadron experience.

The entire squadron would gather one evening in the squadron meeting room, happy to have a few hours off from the war. We were excited to recognize and celebrate the handful of pilots and backseaters who were finishing their twelve-month tour at Da Nang. Since there were between forty and fifty crew members in our squadron, each month we would typically honor the three or four folks headed home to what we called the "real world." We also welcomed the new additions to our unit and, most importantly, recognized the sacrifices of the men lost in action.

Thirty minutes or so before the celebration was scheduled to start, I'd borrow the squadron's truck and pick up three or four nurses from their hootch. The nurses, among the very few American women on the entire base, were always welcomed guests and were treated with great courtesy and respect.

I had been at Da Nang less than a month before learning that a party suit was an absolute necessity for anyone flying fighters in Southeast Asia. The idea of party suits originated with the 357th Tactical Fighter Squadron in Thailand in 1967, and quickly spread to other fighter units. By 1971, even FAC squadrons and other non-fighter units had adopted the custom. More than a sartorial misdemeanor, it was an insult to an honored squadron tradition to show up at a squadron party in anything other than the squadron party suit. Our squadron lived together, fought together, and celebrated together. The party suit was part of the "esprit de corps" of a fighter squadron; the brotherhood of combat, a way of life that dated back to the first fighter squadrons in World War I.

The party suits had the same basic one-piece design as a flight suit, but were made of cotton and were often short-sleeved. Instead of the drab olive Nomex suits that we all wore when flying, each squadron had their own unique color (at the 390th TFS, our party suits were a bright royal blue.) Your rank was embroidered on your shoulders in the usual place, while your name and wings adorned your chest. Patches were added to the shoulders, front, and back of the suit as desired. These patches might include your unit insignia, but more often they carried a humorous meaning, be it a poke at the war effort or a plea to go home.

Our party suits were custom-made by one of those on-the-spot tailors that existed all over Asia. Udorn, Thailand was probably the favorite place to have a suit made. Every couple of weeks, someone from our squadron would ferry a Phantom to Thailand for minor maintenance work. Before leaving, the crew would gather a few basic measurements for anyone who needed a party suit. The tailors were able to take those height, weight, chest, waist, and inseam measurements and create a bespoke masterpiece, all done overnight. The cost was something like $20–25; the patches were a dollar or two extra.

My party suit and I both made it home in one piece from Vietnam, but a few years after my return, my black Labrador retriever got a hold of my party suit and tore it to pieces. I managed to salvage some of the patches, including "Laotian Highway Patrol" (a reference to the near-constant missions over the Ho Chi Minh Trail in the Laotian panhandle), "Ski Mu Gia Pass" (a pass that led from North Vietnam into the Ho Chi Minh trail), "IHTFP" (I Hate This F—ing Place), and "Wild Boars Make Good Lovers" (a reference to the squadron name, the Wild Boars.)

Lord knows who came up with these patches; the humor was brash and sophomoric, but then, fighter squadrons are composed by and large of men in their twenties and thirties, better known for their courage than their sophistication.

A few of the squadron members also wore ostentatious gold chains, bracelets, and other jewelry they'd picked up on trips to Thailand or Hong Kong. Some sported peace symbols worn on a chain around the neck, while others favored jewelry that said "WAR."

The ceremonies began with the Pledge of Allegiance and toasts to our fallen comrades. The departing pilots and backseaters were recognized by the squadron commander and presented with a Gunfighter plaque, a wooden shield with the wing logo in the center and their name and number of combat missions engraved below.

The cocktails, toasts, and wine all seemed to work wonders. Before long, everyone in the room was in a jovial mood, save perhaps the nurses who were beginning to question their attendance at an after-hours event full of drunken men. As the evening wore on, the toasts became more spontaneous, more profane. There were recollections of close calls and near misses, but also tales of how various flyers had gone astray in off-base bars and other places of ill repute. Inevitably, someone on one side of the room would toss a dinner roll at someone on the opposite side of the room, yelling, "Incoming!" A retaliatory strike became the order of the day.

While the food fight raged, someone would crank up a tape deck attached to world-class, ear-splitting speakers. Richie Havens, the Animals, Norman Greenbaum, and other anti-war songs poured from the speakers, played at full blast. The all-time favorite for anyone who ever served in Vietnam was "We've Got to Get Out of This Place." Everyone identified with the lyrics and knew them by heart.

As things got louder and more raucous, the nurses and the squadron commander usually left for safer quarters.

By now, many in the squadron would be operating on a mixture of liquor and false bravado. The energy would ebb and flow, and just when you thought it couldn't get any worse, the time came for the challenge of "carrier landings"—an idea that might seem foolish and dangerous to a sane man, but which seemed perfectly normal to a drunken fighter pilot. The surviving souls would wander out into the corridor that ran the length of the squadron headquarters building, a narrow hallway no more than four feet wide, covered in linoleum. Someone would grab a hose from outside and flood the floor with water. A couple of guys would squat near the end of the corridor with their backs against opposite walls and a rolled towel stretched between them, maybe a foot and a half above the floor.

Although any brave drunken aviator could take a shot at a carrier landing, departing crew members were given preference and strongly encouraged to make an attempt. The "volunteer" would then take a running start, dive on his abdomen, arms extended in front and slightly up, and slide five to ten feet on the wet floor, gliding under the extended towel and raising both legs at the knees to hook the towel. If you came up short of the barrier or slid past without hooking it, you had to do it all over again.

It was mostly harmless fun. Sometimes someone would get a lick on the head, a bruise to the face, or a laceration on the hand. Once, I had to take a pilot to the dispensary to suture his ear.

I'm sure the celebration was against all regulations, but it was part of life in a fighter squadron. Though one of my jobs as a flight surgeon was to encourage flyers to look after their health, I admit that in these instances, I failed miserably.

In a world of rocket attacks and anti-aircraft fire, the squadron party was a nice break from the war.

SEVEN

ANTI-AIRCRAFT FIRE

Summer 1971

IT WASN'T UNTIL my fifth or sixth mission that I saw anti-aircraft fire. I didn't have any preconceived notions of avoiding anti-aircraft artillery, or AAA, as it was called; I knew that if I kept flying, I would encounter it sooner or later. The guys in the squadron were always talking about getting "hosed." It seemed to be one of the main topics of conversation. Every time I flew, the briefing from the intelligence officer mentioned the flights that had faced anti-aircraft fire in the last twenty-four hours. Not everyone got shot at every day, but someone in the wing had always encountered AAA recently. The air war waxed and waned, but it never really stopped; there were no time outs, no days off.

Since no one in our squadron had been shot down since my arrival in country (our first loss would come a few weeks later), AAA seemed more like an abstract concept than a real threat. It was an ill-defined risk, impossible to anticipate. I knew that it was coming eventually, though, and I was anxious to get the experience behind me. It was much like the feeling you have when you know you have to tend to some dreaded chore like a root canal or a colonoscopy; the task lingers there in the back of your mind and you know you'll be better off when you're done with it.

During my entire year in Vietnam, there was always tension between wanting to fly and staying safe. I knew that I wasn't flying as many missions as the other guys, and that gave me a naïve confidence that things would work out for me. There is something liberating about inexperience, I suppose; I didn't know enough to know I was asking for trouble.

The one thing I figured out early on was that if you flew fighters in combat and never got shot at, you hadn't really been at war. You were like a fireman who has never put out a fire or a policeman who had never arrested a criminal. AAA was a dangerous but unavoidable part of flying, the price of admission to the world of fighters. I guess I thought that I would just be up in the sky one day and some nearsighted North Vietnamese gunner would fire up a couple of rounds, and that would be it—mission accomplished. I was just a volunteer backseater; once I had seen AAA, I could check that box, ease back, and take a more relaxed view of combat.

I was flying for the first time with Chuck, a mild-mannered, sandy-haired captain from the Midwest who I rarely saw around the squadron lounge. We were being sent to an area of Steel Tiger (the Laotian panhandle) known as the catcher's mitt. While the Mekong River forms much of the western boundary of the panhandle of Laos, several other rivers flow through the mountains of the interior of the panhandle. From high in the sky, the different areas of jungle and mountain looked remarkably similar; there are no visible roads or villages and few identifying features on the Ho Chi Minh Trail. The flow of the rivers gave a shape and an identity to various locations, so we knew spots in Laos not by their coordinates but by the shapes of the river. The twists and turns created a panoply of images such as the dog's head, the scrotum, and the catcher's mitt.

Chuck was the flight leader for a two-ship interdiction mission; our job was to prevent the flow of supplies as they moved along the Trail and top them from reaching communist forces in South Vietnam, since the rules of engagement still kept North Vietnam off-limits to U.S. air power.

The mission that day was to work with a Forward Air Controller (FAC) on a target in the area of the catcher's mitt. At the pre-flight intelligence briefing, we'd learned that there had been AAA activity around the catcher's mitt for the last several days. This was always unwelcome news; anyone knew that what had already happened several times before was very likely to happen again.

After the briefing, we went to squadron headquarters for flight planning and then headed over to life support to pick up our gear before walking over to the flight line to pre-flight our aircraft.

From the end of the intel briefing to takeoff was usually around an hour and a half. Normally, you would be fairly busy with your gear and checklists, but there was still more than enough time for fear and anxiety to creep in. This was the part of flying in combat that I disliked the most. My spirit of adventure gave way to raw, unadulterated fear. Preparing for the mission was an exercise in anxiety or faith, however you chose to view it.

I think my feelings were the norm, rather than the exception. Many of the guys in my squadron liked to fly Gunfighter alert specifically to minimize the pre-fight anxiety. With Gunfighter alert, two loaded F-4s were kept cocked and ready for tactical emergencies, such as U.S. troops in contact with the enemy or a lucrative target discovered on the Trail. The call would come in to the ready room, and the planes were usually in the air in less than five minutes. Since the crew rushing to get airborne would get the target briefing while taxiing for takeoff, there was less time to spend worrying about the mission.

As I went about my business preparing for takeoff, I was battling a near-paralyzing mix of fear, self-doubt, and apprehension. My brain kept reminding that I was a volunteer. I wasn't required to fly this mission. I wasn't even adding a great deal to the war effort; the North Vietnamese would probably be delighted to face off with an entire air force filled with people of my skill and ability.

I am a wholly different person when I'm scared. By this time, if I could have backed out without losing face, I would have done so. If Chuck was nervous, he was keeping it to himself; his voice was as ordinary as can be, a calm, measured Midwestern twang with no wasted words.

We took off, contacted Hillsboro and got handed off to our FAC. Covey, an OV-10 who worked this area on a regular basis, had found a POL (Petroleum, Oil, Lubricant) storage area that we were supposed to strike. POL is one of those military terms that can mean almost anything, from a large oil storage area or just a few barrels of gasoline. He gave us a standard target briefing—description of the target, direction to attack, position of the bad guys, position of the friendlies (none in the area), direction to head if you're hit, closest base for recovery, etc.

Our flight of two circled in a counter-clockwise direction up around twelve thousand feet, with the FAC down at around four thousand feet. He rolled in to mark the target with his white phosphorous rocket...and then the fireworks began.

Red tracers shot into the sky, arriving mainly in groups of three. It looked as if someone was shooting Roman candles. I saw it first and told Chuck, "Triple A at 3 o'clock."

Chuck answered, "Got it, Doc."

Almost simultaneously, Covey said, "If you've got a fix, you're cleared in on the triple A."

I thought of a thousand things in those first brief seconds. My guts churned, my heart pounded, my whole body felt like it was speaking in tongues. I had a sudden need to be elsewhere; I wished I could just run and hide. It occurred to me that someone else should be doing this, and I cursed myself for having left the security of the dispensary, not mustering the willpower to quit while I was ahead.

This inner soundtrack of self-recrimination continued to play loud and clear for the entire flight.

I remembered the guys in the squadron telling me that it was difficult for AAA to hit a fast mover like a Phantom, but those reassurances seemed to ring hollow in the moment. Sometimes the North Vietnamese would fire their guns into a sector, hoping an aircraft would fly into the saturated area. While I knew that the worst wasn't inevitable, it seemed a lot more plausible than it had a few minutes ago.

The tracers continued to shoot into the sky as multiple puffs of white smoke scattered about like kernels of exploding popcorn. AAA is designed to detonate at a certain altitude if it hasn't struck pay dirt, and those puffs of smoke I was watching fill up the sky were the explosions.

We had briefed making three passes on the target, dropping four MK-82 five hundred pound bombs on each pass. I told myself, *Surely Chuck is going to dump the whole load at once and get us out of here in one piece.* I thought of mentioning this to him, but my mouth was so dry that I probably would have had a hard time speaking.

Chuck rolled left, almost inverted, and headed toward the ground at a 45 degree angle before rolling back upright and pickling off the ordnance. I was a little disappointed to discover that Chuck wasn't thinking what I was thinking. When the bombs came off, it was a normal-feeling release, much like if you'd topped a speed bump in a car. If all twelve bombs had come off at once, it would have felt heavier, more of a heavy jolt than a light tap.

Chuck jinked left and right as we pulled hard, shooting back in to the sky. He must have been getting paid extra to make that Phantom go that fast; we were out of the target area in no time at all.

Back up around twelve thousand feet, number two in our flight rolled in and punched off four bombs. The AAA continued, and we headed down the chute once more. The FAC, holding off and away from the target, said we were doing well. As we made our third pass, I didn't see any more active fire, just the smoke balls from the AAA dissipating into faint wisps, like smoke disappearing from a chimney.

The FAC gave us our BDA (Bomb Damage Assessment); something like, "Two AAA sites possibly destroyed." Who knows; maybe they just got tired of shooting. The FAC didn't drop down real low to confirm the damage, and I didn't blame him one bit.

As we head back to Da Nang, Chuck handed me the controls for a little stick time. I was amazed; his demeanor hadn't changed the whole flight. I, on the other hand, was delighted to have survived the experience. I felt like blurting out, "That AAA was something. I was scared shitless; I thought I was going to die." Instead, I grabbed the controls and did my best to act like the Phantom was my natural second home; that there was no place I'd rather be than flying over the Ho Chi Minh Trail.

We landed and taxied back to the revetment to park the F-4. The crew chief unstrapped me and asked how things went. I told him that we got hosed (I'd recently learned the full meaning of that word and now enjoyed using it).

"Doc," he said, "they can't get you; it's against the rules to shoot a doctor." And he roared with laughter.

Even on quiet days, the walk from the flightline to drop off your gear and debrief never feels routine. But that stroll was one of the best of my life. I felt like I had met an unspoken standard for flying fighters; in my mind, I had taken one for the team. I had that radiant, ineffable joy that comes from having survived combat. It seemed as if God Himself had smiled and patted me on the back. I had taken the challenge, and my soul felt richer for it. There was a feeling of satisfaction and accomplishment, a sense of completeness, a sense of relief. I had never experienced anything in my life that was simultaneously as gratifying and as terrifying.

I couldn't wait to do it again.

EIGHT

LOST IN ACTION

September 30, 1971

RON BOND'S AIRCRAFT went down over the Ho Chi Minh Trail in Laos on September 30, 1971. He was the first man from the 390th Tactical Fighter Squadron to be lost in combat since my arrival in Vietnam.

Ron was in the backseat of Stormy 3 on a fast FAC (Forward Air Controller) mission, piloted by Mike Donovan from the 421st TFS. The F-4, operating alone, was on a visual reconnaissance mission over the Trail, looking for targets in a high-risk area. Stormy 3 took off shortly after daylight and spent the morning scouring the jungle at a low altitude, looking for signs of enemy activity. The Phantom had completed two aerial refuelings from a KC-135 tanker over Thailand when it was last heard from, shortly before noon.

When Stormy 3 failed to report later in the day, search and rescue (SAR) efforts began immediately. Rescue aircraft were sent over the last known areas of operation, looking for a downed plane, a parachute, radio calls, any sign of the men or their aircraft. Every hour was critical; since the aircraft almost certainly went down in enemy territory, the chances of rescue decreased with time. Each day, the SAR mission continued without success.

Finally, on October 6, nearly a week later, a suspected wreckage was found in a jungle valley in one of the worst areas of Steel Tiger. The spot was too dangerous to insert ground troops for positive identification. Ron Bond and Mike Donovan were listed as Missing in Action (MIA).

The flight of Stormy 3 was no ordinary mission. Normally, an FAC is a slower aircraft that loiters over an area of responsibility looking for targets such as trucks, fuel depots, or weapons caches. The FAC directs the fast moving fighters, marking the target with a smoke rocket and coordinating the details of the strike. Afterward, the FAC takes a good look at the target and give a bomb damage assessment (BDA). Were some trucks, weapons, or fuel dumps destroyed, were some roads or bridges knocked out, or were there just a few more holes in the jungle? This is how the score was kept in Vietnam.

Some areas, however, were too dangerous for a regular FAC to work in—areas where there were too many anti-aircraft guns or surface-to-air missiles (SAMs). Since a slow FAC would not be able to survive in a dangerous zone, you needed a fast mover to find targets for other fast movers. The crews that flew these fast FAC sorties had one of the most dangerous jobs in the Air Force. Mike and Ron were part of an elite volunteer program that accepted only the best pilots and backseaters. They flew in high threat areas, places too dangerous for anything but the fast movers.

Stormy was the call sign of the fast FACs of the 366th TFW at Da Nang. The program started in 1968, and eventually most F-4 wings in Southeast Asia had a fast FAC component, each with their own call sign. "Wolf" FACs worked out of the 8th TFW; "Laredo" FACs were part of the 432nd TRW; "Tiger" FACs belonged to the

388th TFW. But regardless of moniker, the men who flew these missions were the bravest of the brave.

Ron Bond lived three doors down the hall from me. He had been in country for nearly eight months and had already logged a hundred and forty-nine combat missions. The fact that he was in the Stormy program meant that he was one of the top GIBs in the wing. Short and stockily built, Ron was a high school wrestler and an Air Force Academy graduate. I remember him as a man who took his job seriously, a man who loved flying, a man who knew what he was doing.

I first learned about Ron's loss the afternoon he went missing, when I returned from a mission. The intelligence officer told us that Stormy 3 was hours overdue. At the time, the information was fragmented and incomplete, but we could fill in the blanks. The fact that the crew hadn't been seen or heard from was a bad sign.

Making matters worse, Stormy 3 was alone. Fighters rarely worked alone; normally, if an F-4 was shot down, there was a wingman or a regular FAC who could look for a parachute, get a fix on the location, and initiate the search and rescue. Everyone knew that if you survived a crash, the Air Force would risk everything to get you out, but they had to first find a starting point, be it a parachute or a crash site.

No resource was spared in the SAR effort to locate and recover Stormy 3. The guys in the squadron continued to fly a full schedule; everyone hung on and hoped for the best. I'm not sure if the searches stopped once the suspected wreckage was found, but our hopes grew dimmer with each passing day.

Several weeks later, I lent a hand as Ron's roommate packed Ron's personal belongings for shipment to his family back home. In a way, cleaning out his room seemed to add a certain finality to his loss.

Ron Bond remained MIA until 1979, when his status was administratively changed to killed in action (KIA). His remains have never been recovered. Ron was single, but his family suffered through decades of trials and tribulations fighting the military bureaucracy trying to definitively determine his fate. Their hope never died.

The great fear of every military family is to see a group of officers come to their front door. During the year I served at Hurlburt Field in Florida, I once had to accompany the squadron commander and the chaplain as we notified a wife that her husband had been killed in a stateside airplane crash. It's a sad but necessary job; a personal visit is much better than a telegram or phone call. Because of his concern for his mother's health, Ron had listed his older brother as the person to contact. The family later gathered as a group to break the news to his mother.

Wartime doesn't lend itself to grief counseling. There was no time allotted for mourning, no discussion of the various stages of grief, no worry about survival guilt. Loss is visceral and unspoken. By 1971, everyone who signed up to fly fighters in combat was well aware of the danger of being killed or captured. Our missions were flown as before; there was no easing up, no change in tactics. But things were quieter and more reserved for a while; there was less of the back-and-forth banter, the relentless kidding that usually took place during the evening poker games. I spent the next few days hanging around the squadron lounge, quietly raising the subject of Ron's loss in case anyone wanted to talk about it.

Every time we briefed a flight, everyone was urged to "fly smart." These words were a hollow effort at reassuring ourselves. There was no guarantee that being careful would keep you alive; there was nothing to suggest Stormy 3 hadn't "flown smart."

There are times in war when courage isn't rewarded. The reality was that the Vietnam War was a potentially lethal place for people who flew fighters. North Vietnam, Laos, South Vietnam, Cambodia—you could get killed anywhere in Southeast Asia. More than five hundred F-4s were lost during the war, about one out of every eight Phantoms made for the U.S. If you flew F-105 Thunderchiefs, the odds were even worse. Some forty percent of the "Thuds" manufactured were lost in combat, mostly over North Vietnam. It was an unspoken fact that every time you took off, there was a distinct possibility that you wouldn't be coming back. The courage to face these risks, not once or twice but on a daily basis, is what I most admired about the members of my squadron.

At the end of my tour, another Stormy fast FAC Phantom from my squadron was shot down, both crew members KIA. In the strikes over North Vietnam between Christmas and New Year's in 1971, a 390th F-4 was hit, but both crew members ejected and were rescued. Another squadron Phantom was lost at the battle of An Loc in April 1972; fortunately, both of the crew were picked up.

Ron Bond was one of many American men who paid the ultimate price in the service of our country. I greatly admired his skill, courage, and sacrifice.

NINE

LIFE IN A FIGHTER SQUADRON

1971–1972

LIVING WITH A fighter squadron in wartime was nothing like I'd imagined it would be. Living together and sharing the risk of combat created a common bond among the squadron members. In some ways, it was like residing in a college dorm, save that most of the students were in their twenties or thirties instead of their teens. People came and went at all hours of the day, you could always find a bull session somewhere, and there was no shortage of alcohol.

If you ignored the sandbags lining the outer walls, the accommodations at our squadron barracks even looked a lot like a college residence hall from the 1960s. We paid a couple of middle-aged Vietnamese women out of our own pockets to do the cleaning and laundry. We called our accommodations our "hootch," a word that came to be applied to most any living quarters in Southeast Asia.

That said, there were a few key differences between life in a fighter squadron and life in a college dorm. Instead of concentrating on studying and graduating, the focus was on flying fighters, completing missions, and staying alive. These men were no innocents brought to war; everyone at Da Nang had already been out and about in the world. Their goal wasn't to receive a diploma or get a job; their challenge was to finish their twelve month tour and return home to their families alive.

By the time I arrived, the living conditions for a fighter squadron were a long way from the Spartan lifestyle seen in the early days of the war. As a result, though the food was horrible and my family was absent, I still had many of the comforts of home. If it hadn't have been for the rocket attacks and the anti-aircraft fire, it would have seemed like a summer camp for grown men.

But perhaps it would be more accurate to compare it to a school for civil servants. As an outsider, what struck me immediately was the vast amount of paperwork generated during wartime. There were several layers of bureaucracy, and each one needed a written report using the stilted language common to the military. The Air Force went to war and the paper pushers came along for the ride; the system was a self-replicating bureaucracy. Even at Da Nang, there were a lot of people who placed more emphasis on following rules and regulations than on accomplishing the mission. I knew this was true in the United States, but I thought it might be different in a war zone.

In addition to flying, everyone in the squadron had other assigned jobs—tasks like safety officer, scheduling officer, weapons officer, housing officer, etc. Since I had my regular job as a physician at the dispensary, I fought through paperwork on the medical end and had few assigned squadron chores. (Though, if we had a meeting of the full squadron, I usually tried to attend, as this often meant something major was about to happen.)

The fighter crews of the Vietnam era were all male. These men loved and valued flying and felt they were part of a unique brotherhood, an elite group. There was a certain amount of machismo and panache, and a more than a bit of swaggering adventurism, but that has always been part of a fighter squadron's culture. I know a lot has changed in the military during the last half-century, but during the Vietnam War, a fighter squadron was no place for a woman.

Around half of the men in our squadron were married, but there were enough single men to ensure that the local bars never lacked for customers. Occasionally, a crew would ferry a Phantom to Thailand or Taipei for maintenance and expose themselves to all the sins of the Orient. If you were lucky enough to go, you were required to return with a story of good food and good times. I was no stranger to the late night knock on my door, and was sometimes called upon to offer a clandestine consultation about some malady of the groin. Treating venereal disease has always been a staple of military medicine, especially in wartime.

Many of the guys spent a fair amount of their free time drinking beer and playing cards at the Boar's Head Inn, our unit's lounge located in the squadron headquarters building. Despite its grand-sounding name, in reality the Inn was a real bare-bones operation; just a few tables and chairs, a couple of sofas, a small bar, and a refrigerator full of beer. A mounted boar's head hung over the bar, and the squadron and wing insignias graced the walls. A seldom-used, toaster-sized television set was stuck high in the corner of the room.

And that wasn't the least of the Boar's Head's limitations; there were no waitresses and no food. If you needed a drink, you helped yourself and left a quarter in the kitty. Every few weeks, someone would borrow several ration cards, grab the squadron truck, and head to the Base Exchange to restock. The person who did this job was considered one of the most important men in the squadron and was subject to immediate criticism for any failure to perform his duty.

The squadron had a movie projector, and each night we could watch a different film. The movies, mainly third-rate films by people you had never heard of, rotated among the three fighter squadrons. I had always considered fighter pilots as the modern day version of the strong and silent cowboy and, sure enough, the squadron's taste in movies confirmed my opinion—westerns were always popular.

The nightly poker games were serious, albeit low-stakes, contests. The rules were bizarre, with a variety of high-low, split pots and multiple wild cards. The hardest job I had was keeping up with the changing rules. If I had a lucky night, I might win enough to eat out at the local Chinese restaurant. If I lost, I figured I was saving my good fortune for more important things.

This was a men's group, so the topics of conversation were predictable—flying, women, sports, and politics, in that order. With the exception of flying, these subjects have probably occupied men's minds since the beginning of time.

Fighter pilots love talking about airplanes almost as much as they love flying them. For these men, the war was a great opportunity. They had generally finished near the top of their pilot training class and were flying the best fighter aircraft in the world in the biggest war of the day. The F-4 was the high end of the Air Force hierarchy, the top rung of the ladder. For fighter pilots, flying was life and life was flying; it seemed like they couldn't get enough of it. They had a true love affair with fighters, while I had more of a platonic relationship.

The conversations tended to revolve around the pros and cons of different aircraft, the close calls they'd had, the tricks of the trade, the deadly screw-ups. There were plenty of tall tales, breathless misadventures, and charming misfortunes. The stories were usually overflowing with bravado; the squadron bar was a clearinghouse of fighter pilot lore. I mostly listened and tried to learn. I was careful to avoid asking questions that would expose the large gaps in my knowledge of flying, but I found that if I said something like, "Tell me how that happened," and listened carefully, I could learn a lot.

I always reminded myself that this was a group of men drinking beer; no one was under oath, and what really happened was probably exaggerated.

The military life is a transient one. Many of our squadron members grew up in military families and had been stationed around the world for most of their lives. Since you're never in one spot for very long, it's almost impossible to be a devoted sports fan. You get moved from place to place, and you rarely get a chance to watch your team on television, much less in person. (We had several Naval Academy graduates who kept up with the Army-Navy rivalry, but the interest didn't seem as intense for Air Force Academy graduates.)

In the Vietnam era, professional baseball was still the most popular sport, and the New York Yankees seemed to have the most followers. In pro football, the Dallas Cowboys were the top team. No matter who you liked, you stayed in touch the best you could. But with a roughly twelve hour time difference back home, you never saw a real live game while stationed in Vietnam.

If sports were difficult to follow in wartime, the ebb and flow of political events were even worse. A fighter squadron is by necessity an apolitical group, as removed from national politics as an organization can be. Everyone in our squadron loved his country and was proud to serve in wartime, but the main reason that they were in the Air Force was that they loved to fly. The opportunity to soar in the sky was an adventure that they were proud to choose. An Air Force squadron has virtually no say in strategy and no input in political goals; its duty is simply to perform the mission it is assigned, regardless of the danger or difficulty. A fighter squadron in wartime is the place where political plans become actions, the spot where the dangerous work gets done; the one place where you are defined by what you do rather than what you say.

Even though their lives were often at the mercy of politicians, most of the men in my squadron cared little for politics. They were probably more conservative than the general public, but they rarely identified themselves as Republican or Democrat. Most of them had only had the chance to vote on a few occasions. After all, they were constantly on the move, often being assigned with little notice to another base in another country.

So despite being in the line of fire, the political controversies of the Vietnam War that seemed so important back home were rarely discussed at Da Nang. Stories of war protestors in the U.S. would occasionally filter in through magazines and newspapers, but by 1971–1972, this was old news that garnered little notice. Everyone agreed that it was more fun to protest a war than to fight it. In early 1972, when Richard Nixon went to Red China, his visit meant very little to the 390th TFS. There was no cease-fire; not even a slowdown in the pace of the war. In fact, Nixon's trip was followed by the launching of a spring offensive by the North Vietnamese, and the air war actually got ratcheted up a notch.

The men doing the fighting were committed to carrying out their mission, regardless of who was setting policy. No matter who was serving as President, anything less than a total commitment is an unaffordable luxury during wartime. This is the way the military has always worked; you fall in line and you follow orders.

Still, the people who flew had definite opinions about the men who served as their commanders-in-chief. Lyndon Johnson was almost universally disliked by anyone who flew in combat in Southeast Asia. The President had launched the Rolling Thunder air campaign in March 1965. At the time, it seemed like a good idea. Air strikes in North Vietnam would persuade Hanoi to drop their support of the Viet Cong insurgents in the South, while destroying the bridges, rail yards, and power plants in the North would reduce the men and materiel headed to South Vietnam. Our South Vietnamese allies would realize that we were committed to helping them survive as an independent nation. LBJ and his civilian advisors clearly thought they had things pretty well figured out.

The problem came when, early in the conflict, Johnson's military advisors presented him with a plan to strike the major targets in the North in a brief, intense bombing campaign, but Johnson, fearful of Chinese intervention in the war, instead chose a limited, gradualist approach. The President (along with his Secretary of Defense and Secretary of State) would pick and choose the targets to be struck. Fancying themselves military tacticians, they would select the number of aircraft to be sent, the types of plane (no bombers allowed, just fighters carrying bombs), the types of ordnance, and the routes to be flown to and from the target. Their target selection was good for a limited number of days. If the weather was bad, it was tough luck for the Air Force; the military had to request permission again.

To give LBJ some credit, the threat of Chinese intervention in the war was real. One only need look back fifteen years to the Korean War to see that. And the President, as Commander-in-Chief, has always set military strategy, but the level of civilian-tactical control during Rolling Thunder was unprecedented. Some of the rules of engagement seemed designed to produce failure. Many areas, such as central Hanoi and Haiphong, were completely off-limits. At times, pilots were prohibited from striking SAM sites or MiG bases unless they were first shot at. During the three years of the Rolling Thunder campaign, Johnson would occasionally call a halt to the bombing, allowing the North Vietnamese to regroup and resupply their forces, all of which worked to the detriment of the war effort.

As is usually the case, it was the young men chosen to fight the old men's battles that suffered the consequences. The fighter crews, the ones who were actually risking their lives, resented being hand-cuffed by byzantine rules of engagement cooked up by inept politicians. These political restrictions cost American lives and took a toll in captured airmen. In North Vietnam, the majority of POWs were fighter crews shot down over the North during the Rolling Thunder campaign.

Of course, this was all before my time. When I came to Da Nang in 1971, the Rolling Thunder campaign had been over for more than two years, and with just a few exceptions, North Vietnam was a prohibited area. But for the members of my squadron, those POWs were never forgotten. There was often a personal link; some of our pilots had trained under some of the POWs or had served with them at another base, and they often knew their families. The POWs weren't statistics; they were friends, neighbors, and ac-quaintances with wives and children.

Most of the pilots in my squadron felt that Johnson's leadership in the war was a story of foolish rules and squandered opportuni-ties that resulted in an unnecessarily large number of airmen being killed or captured over North Vietnam. There was also a lot of re-sentment over the fact that the President had stayed mostly silent on the fate of the POWs, even though he had evidence that they had been tortured. While he claimed to be working behind the scenes to free them, the whole issue seemed to be an embarrass-ment for his administration. The POWs were a living, breathing symbol of the failure of his Vietnam policies.

I understood and agreed with most of the criticisms of Johnson and his policies. After all, the warriors who flew the fighters over North

Vietnam, battling AAA, SAMs, and MiGs, were living, breathing heroes to me. I couldn't help but be influenced by their sentiments. But there was another reason, of which I was totally unaware at the time, for LBJ being held in such low regard by many in the military. During World War II, Johnson had been awarded the Army Silver Star for gallantry by General Douglas McArthur. But his decoration was an outright sham, a clear case of stolen valor and an insult to the brave men who earned the honor.

At the time of Pearl Harbor, Johnson was a politically ambitious Texas congressman. Since the voters of that era frowned on politicians who sat out the war in Washington, Johnson felt that he needed wartime service on his resume, and so he persuaded President Roosevelt to send him on an inspection tour of the Pacific. In this way, LBJ managed to tag along as an observer on a single bombing mission in a B-26 over New Guinea in 1942. The B-26, according to one version of events, was attacked by enemy fighters; others deny that an attack ever took place. Regardless, before his aircraft reached the target, a generator went out and the plane was forced to turn back.

LBJ was nothing more than an idle passenger during this mission, merely along for the ride. Nonetheless, he received the Silver Star, along with a citation stating that he had shown "marked coolness" during the flight. The whole episode had lasted no more than thirteen minutes according to most accounts, and none of the other crewmembers received any decoration. Later revelations by surviving crewmembers suggested that the aircraft never even came under fire.

Johnson's Silver Star has to be one of the most undeserved decorations ever awarded. Lyndon Johnson placed a lot of restrictions on the men fighting the Vietnam War, but he never had any reservations when it came to wearing his bogus Silver Star. For most of his life, he wore a Silver Star pin on his lapel, and frequently boasted to others about his courage under fire.

Although this episode of the bogus Silver Star was news to me, I could certainly see why a fighter squadron resented an unearned military decoration. No one gets rich or famous serving in the armed forces; one of the few rewards of military service is recognition for courage and valor in combat. Most everyone who flew fighters on Southeast Asia won multiple Air Medals. When I was at Da Nang, there was even a formula for awarding the Air Medal for fighter combat missions, based on the danger involved. Ten missions were needed over North Vietnam, fifteen missions in Laos, or twenty missions in South Vietnam. Since most of the pilots and WSOs had more than a hundred and fifty combat missions during a tour, the Air Medal was often earned multiple times.

In addition, almost every pilot and WSO in a fighter squadron earned a Distinguished Flying Cross during their tour. If you flew enough missions, you were sure to encounter your share of dangerous sorties. In fact, the squadron had an awards officer whose job it was to keep track of these particularly hazardous missions. But the Silver Star was rarely awarded; our squadron had perhaps a handful of people who had earned the nation's third highest decoration for truly heroic conduct under very heavy enemy fire. And unlike LBJ, no one received a Silver Star for tagging along in the back of an airplane.

I never heard anyone talk or brag about their military decorations. During my year in Vietnam, that wasn't part of the culture of a fighter squadron. Self-effacement was very common, but self-promotion was hardly ever seen. A flight suit had no room for military awards. That isn't to say we didn't respect those who had achieved recognition; our wing was the home of Captain Lance Sijan, the first Air Force Academy graduate to receive the Congressional Medal of Honor. Sijan was shot down over Laos in November 1967. In spite of multiple fractures, no food, and little water, he evaded capture for forty-six days.

Richard Nixon, on the other hand, was seen as a stronger and more decisive leader, and was therefore held in higher regard as Commander-in-Chief than was LBJ. His Vietnamization policy was welcome in our squadron; we were all glad to see an unpopular war wind down. From a practical point of view, the reduction in ground forces made little difference to most of us. Serving in Vietnam was sort of like being pregnant; you either are or you are not. It didn't matter if there were only sixty thousand other Americans serving with you instead of five hundred thousand; you were still personally one hundred percent at risk.

More importantly, Nixon took on the POW issue, bringing the account of the prisoners and their treatment to the forefront. In a war that had yet to produce a fighter ace, these POWs became our heroes, a rallying point for the country. Nixon's treatment of the POW problem won him many admirers in our squadron.

Admittedly, the vagaries of politics were just window dressing in Vietnam. Regardless of who was the commander-in-chief, regardless of anyone's personal political persuasion, the job of a fighter squadron has always been to fly the assigned mission. These men faced danger and death every time they flew. They did what the mission demanded and never complained. The fact that they were trained to do so made it no less courageous.

TEN

AIR-TO-AIR REFUELING

Fall 1971

I HAD BEEN flying for around three months when I was fragged on a single ship mission to Cambodia.

One-aircraft missions were rare; our squadron almost always worked in flights of two planes. Trips to Cambodia were even rarer, as most of our targets were in Laos and South Vietnam. I was happy to be flying with my buddy, Ben—a big, husky bear of a guy with a permanent grin on his face. Ben was one of those people who did everything right and made it look effortless. He also had the ability to find that touch of the absurd, which never seemed far from the surface in wartime. Ben rarely seemed worried, and that tended to rub off on me.

Our target that day was a weapons cache just over the South Vietnamese border. As I was checking out the details at the mission planning room at wing headquarters, I noticed that our flight had an air-to-air refueling scheduled on the way to the target. This was something completely new for me; I had never experienced an air-to-air refueling in any aircraft.

During most day missions out of Da Nang, we rarely had to refuel. The Ho Chi Minh Trail was just a few minutes away by air; by the time we had taken off, checked in with the Airborne Command and Control Center, and contacted our Forward Air Controller, we had usually crossed the fence into the Laotian panhandle. Once our squadron switched to nights (the three squadrons rotated night flying duties), the story changed. The night missions were flown in support of gunships over the Ho Chi Minh Trail, and two or three air-to-air refueling on each mission were the norm.

Although the first aerial refueling in combat took place during the Korean War, Vietnam is rightly known as the first tanker war. Since a flying gas station was available, fighters could take off with more ordnance and less fuel and could stay airborne longer, greatly extending their range. During Rolling Thunder (and later, during the Linebacker campaign), aircraft would hit the tanker on the way into North Vietnam and, if necessary, refuel again on the way home. Wartime is full of emergencies, and those tankers came to the rescue of many fighters away from home and short on fuel. There were even a few times when they broke the rules and ventured into enemy airspace to save an aircraft from flameout.

At the time of my mission with Ben, our squadron hadn't flown at night for several months; I wondered if this single-plane trip to Cambodia might have been an effort to keep refueling skills sharp. Since I didn't want to screw anything up, I asked Ben if there was anything I needed to know, anything I ought to do to prepare for the aerial refueling.

"Hell, no, Doc," he replied. "The tanker is a flying gas station. We'll drive up, tell the attendant to fill it up, and watch while he pumps the gas. We won't even need a credit card. Those guys are very talented; they really know how to pass gas." Then he burst out laughing. The other pilots in the room smiled and shook their heads. I was the fall guy for one of the oldest lines in the Air Force.

A little over twenty minutes after takeoff, we were on a tanker track over Thailand. The big KC-135 tankers flew in Northern Thailand, just over the Laotian border, maintaining a certain altitude and direction. These oblong orbits were called "tracks," and most had a call sign with the name of a color, such as cherry, lemon, or orange. We headed toward our scheduled rendezvous with the Cherry tanker. As we approached the tanker, another F-4 was disconnecting from the refueling boom while a second Phantom was waiting off to the side for his turn. The scene reminded me of a mother duck with three ducklings in tow.

The KC-135 dwarfed the F-4s in size. The aircraft was a big, lumbering giant of a plane, a modified Boeing 707 that could deliver many thousands of pounds of fuel to other aircraft and still have plenty left to fly around for hours.

The second aircraft was cleared in for fuel and connected to the boom in no time at all. After another few minutes, it was our turn. I thought there might be a bit more to it than Ben had described, and I was right, but the whole process was very orderly and methodical; just a few words exchanged between the pilot and the tanker. Ben flew our aircraft under and slightly behind the belly of the tanker, where a series of lights on the bottom of the fuselage let him know when he was positioned properly. I watched as the boom operator in the KC-135 lay on his stomach, peering through a Plexiglas window, moving the boom as he gave us directions over the radio. His instructions were short and specific: "Left two feet," "Up one foot," etc.

The boom is a long pipe attached to the rear of the tanker that telescopes in and out. Near the end of the boom are two airfoils that angle out in a V shape. They give stability to the device and allow the boomer to "fly" the boom. The refueling receptacle on an F-4 is on the spine of the plane, just behind the canopy of the backseater.

The fighter pilot's job during refueling is to fly a stable position within the air refueling envelope. Too close is dangerous—in rare instances, mid-air collisions have occurred—too far back, and the boomer is forced to disconnect. It's a dynamic process; both aircraft are flying more than three hundred miles per hour, constantly moving in three dimensions, up and down, back and forth, left and right. To me, it seemed like they were bouncing about on separate, unsynchronized trampolines. It's similar in some ways to flying close formation on another fighter's wing; it looks routine to the uninitiated, but is often more difficult than it appears.

I watched as the boom flailed around like a drunken snake. For a moment, it looked like I was going to get popped on the head by the end of the boom, but we had a good boom operator who made a fast connection. A few minutes after hookup, he told us that he was disconnecting and that we had gotten such-and-such thousand pounds of fuel. (A gallon of fuel is a little over 6.5 pounds; a Phantom burns a heck of a lot of gas.)

I wrote down the number of pounds of fuel we had taken from the tanker. This was my sole contribution to the refueling process.

Most of the fighter pilots I flew with seemed to take air-to-air refueling for granted. They did it at night, they did it in bad weather, they did it whenever it was called for. It was like taking off and landing; a skill that every fighter pilot has. They made a difficult task seem ordinary.

I was impressed. For me, this was yet another one of those small miracles that makes flying fighters such a great experience.

ELEVEN

DOOM CLUB

1971–1972

I HADN'T BEEN at Da Nang very long before I discovered the officers' club, officially known as the DOOM club (Da Nang Officers' Open Mess).

Officer clubs are a staple of military installations around the world, a welcome spot to meet, eat, and drink; a temporary refuge from the trials and tribulations of wartime. Admittedly, whoever named the club at Da Nang had a macabre, twisted sense of humor. I already felt jinxed, if not cursed, by being shipped to Southeast Asia; I didn't need to be reminded of my lot in life every time I had a drink.

The DOOM club, located several miles from our squadron headquarters, was too far to walk to, especially during the monsoon season. If I wanted to visit the club, I had to catch a ride. Most of the time, I would tag along with a few of the guys from my squadron. If we were lucky, we could borrow one of the squadron's trucks; otherwise, we had to hitchhike.

When you're accustomed to being catered to in a jet aircraft, being forced to thumb a ride in a monsoon downpour can be a little bit of a letdown. At Da Nang, the ground transportation network was a true democratic system, one that worked well. In the military, officers and enlisted men live in different worlds most of the time, but when it came to catching a ride, everyone was treated equally—first come first served, with no deference to rank. If you were driving a vehicle and had room for passengers, you were obligated to stop and pick up anyone with their thumb out. Even the wing commander had to play by the rules; on several occasions, he picked me up and went out of his way to drop me at the front door of the club.

The DOOM club, located in an old wooden frame building with a tin roof, looked like it had been built before Ho Chi Minh was born. The writing on the sign out front had that pseudo-Trader Vic's look that suggested you were about to enter a Polynesian paradise.

The reality was far different. The main door was manned by a middle-age Vietnamese woman who was tough as hell. She had seen American officers come and go for years, and the fact that you flew fighters in combat did not impress her in the least. Her main purpose in life was to make sure that you had paid your club dues. It was a cruel system; if you had missed coming to the club the previous month, you still had to pay the dues for that month as well as the current one. No one was exempt from her scrutiny; if the squadron commander had not paid up, he could not enter.

I joined the DOOM club soon after I arrived, but my account was always in arrears. I was frugal to the point of cheapness, and really hated paying money for past dues. The iron lady seemed to take a special delight when I was forced to shell out for several missed months. I sometimes wondered if she worked for the Viet Cong.

The main room was dark and cool, with a low ceiling and a long bar at one end. Nearby, a bell hung on the wall. Bells are found in most military drinking spots; when it was rung, it was always good news: it indicated that someone was buying a round. Adjacent to the bar were some tables and a dance floor. Most of the time, a jukebox provided the background music, but occasionally the club would bring in a band from the Philippines. The DOOM club's dance floor was generous, but lacked the one critical element needed for a successful dance—women. Only officers were allowed in the club, and there weren't that many female officers stationed at Da Nang.

Posted on one wall was a handmade list that had been added to many times over the years. The topic under discussion was, "Why an F-4 is Better than a Woman." The opinions were a little wry and very predictable. "A Phantom doesn't come with in-laws;" "A Phantom doesn't mind if you look at other airplanes;" "A Phantom can be flown any time of the month;" "A Phantom can be turned on by simply flipping a switch." The list seemed longer every time I visited the club. This conversation, and others like it, has probably been going on since the time of the Wright brothers—the humor of lonely men away from home, missing their loved ones.

Officers in all the services—Army, Navy, Marine, and Air Force—showed up at the club. Some pilots were in for a few days of temporary duty; others had had to recover at Da Nang because of weather or aircraft problems. Everyone tended to hang out with their own squadron members, but often there would be animated discussions over who had the worst lot in the war. It all depended on your point of view. The crews from the bases in Thailand were mocked for living in a spot with good food, bars, women, and no rocket attacks. Army and Marine officers who lived and worked in the field felt that we were living in paradise; compared to their days in the jungle, Da Nang Air Base was heaven.

I always made a special point to visit the DOOM club on those occasions when we celebrated the final mission of one or more of our squadron members. At the end of a crew's last mission, their Phantom would taxi back to the revetment, followed by a parade of base vehicles. The lucky men would be hosed down by a fire truck and a bottle of champagne would be popped for a well-earned goodbye toast. That same evening, the fortunate ones would, by tradition, come to the DOOM club to buy a round for the house. The happiness and relief of someone who has flown one hundred and fifty or more combat missions and survived to return home was almost palpable. Frugal as I was, I still looked forward to the day when it was my time to buy drinks for the house.

The final mission celebrations at the DOOM club were unpredictable and sometimes chaotic; often I had no choice but to relax and have a good time. A fighter squadron gets used to running in high gear, and even relaxation can turn into a remarkably intense experience. Some of the men were prone to drink hard and drink often. The prevailing sentiment seemed to be that there would be time later on for clean, safe living.

During the first half of my tour, martinis were the drink of choice. (I have no idea who started the trend, and fortunately it faded away about six months later.) When it was someone's turn to buy, that's what got bought. The call to the bartender was, "A round of silver bullets for the whole table."

I've always hated martinis. But, since that was what was being served, and since the price was right (and since I really hated not drinking a free drink), that's what I drank. If I could manage to slip away after no more than one or two, I did fine. If I succumbed to a third or fourth, I usually ended up welded to the bar for the rest of the evening. If you drink enough, dinner ceases to matter very much. (But then, the DOOM club was always more of a drinking spot than a place to eat; the food was too expensive to make a regular habit of dining out.) Eventually, I would wander out of the dark, air-conditioned club into the sweltering heat and humidity and head home, happy that my friends had survived a year at Da Nang, hoping that I would survive the night.

On some evenings, when the alcohol seemed to flow like the Mekong River, we would all talk about the fortunes of war. The Vietnam War was a mixed bag for many people; it had its good moments, but they were usually far outweighed by the bad. The war was different things for different people at different times; danger and discomfort were not evenly distributed.

For most Americans, the image of Vietnam is based on television reports, movies, and newspaper accounts mixed with stories from the veterans who served. The usual picture is one of young soldiers and marines on patrol in the jungle, fierce firefights, helicopters rushing troops into battle and lifting out the wounded, refugees streaming from burning villages. The common view is that a near-constant struggle with death and destruction on every side was the lot of every Vietnam soldier.

This role, that of the heroic grunt on patrol battling the elusive Viet Cong guerilla, represented at most a quarter of the troops who served in Vietnam. The vast majority of veterans worked in supporting roles—not completely out of danger, but in relative comfort. The United States military did its best to make its rear bases as comfortable as possible. This was especially true of the Air Force. Most of the big air bases were near the coast and were well-defended and well-supplied with base exchanges, barracks, and entertainment. The longer the war lasted, the more elaborate the facilities became. Clean sheets and cold beer were the norm for many of us in Vietnam.

That said, there was no rear line in Vietnam, no place of absolute safety. Everyone was vulnerable to some kind of attack, be it from rockets, mortars, or street bombs. At Da Nang, we were hit at least a dozen times by rockets attacks. Some were harmless, some killed people. It wasn't nearly as dangerous as the siege of Khe Sanh or many of the other battles fought by the Marines, but that's little solace to the families of the people who died from a random rocket.

Life in a fighter squadron was even more tenuous. The possibility of death or imprisonment was there every time you flew. One evening you'll be having a drink in the officers' club with a friend; the next day, he's shot down over the Ho Chi Minh Trail. There were no guarantees for anyone.

Like life itself, the Vietnam War was unfair; some were killed and maimed, others had little to worry about. We were resigned to the war, and we all agreed that you have no choice but to deal with life as it comes along. Sometimes you're dealt a good hand, sometimes you're not. If you're fortunate and get to work in the mess hall instead of going on patrol in the jungle, give thanks. If things turn bad, as often happens, do the best that you can.

Anyone who serves a tour in a war zone, regardless of the danger, deserves our thanks. Only around ten percent of the American men of draft age served in Vietnam. I found spending a year away from my family to be a horrible experience. I had been married less than two years when I left for Da Nang, and my son was only nine months old. When I go back and read the letters that I sent my wife from Vietnam, they reveal the pain and loneliness of that separation, the kind that comes when the most important people in your life are no longer a part of your daily existence.

TWELVE

NIGHT MOVES

1971–1972

THE 366TH TACTICAL Fighter Wing was composed of three squadrons of F-4 Phantoms. Normally, two of the three squadrons flew day missions, while the third one handled the night duties. Roughly every two months or so, word would come down from wing headquarters and the rotation would change. A different squadron would move to nights, while the crews returning to daytime would breathe a sigh of relief, happy to reenter the "normal" world of flying fighters in combat.

Flying at nights was hard. The missions were longer, multiple air-to-air refuelings were the rule, and poor vision made even routine tasks difficult. I logged only a handful of night sorties, but they were some of the most challenging missions I was ever flew. More than enough to make me appreciate and admire the men who flew them night after night.

Regardless of whether we flew at night or during the day, our wing had the same basic mission: interdiction of the weapons and supplies coming down the Ho Chi Minh Trail in Laos. The goal was always the same, but the types of aircraft, the tactics, and the success rate varied greatly between day and night.

Interdiction was a weak part of a weak strategy used by the United States in Vietnam. The goal wasn't to cut the Trail, or to completely stop the flow of men and materiel to the communists in the South; that had already been tried before, unsuccessfully. We were attempting to slow the movement, to make the Ho Chi Minh Trail more costly to the North Vietnamese, to reduce the pressure on the South Vietnamese.

It was a flawed strategy, none of things that are normally done to win a war were allowed. The supplies for the North Vietnamese and their Viet Cong brethren came in mostly by ship at Haiphong. The Rolling Thunder bombing campaign of North Vietnam had ended in 1968, so during my tour the trucks loaded with war materiel rolled mostly unimpeded through North Vietnam before entering the trail via one of the mountain passes linking North Vietnam and Laos. Yet invading North Vietnam was forbidden, mining Haiphong harbor was off-limits, and sending American troops into Laos was prohibited.

Everyone in the squadron knew that waging war with a nebulous goal like "peace with honor" was a difficult task, but no one complained. As I've said, a fighter squadron's job is to perform the mission assigned. It's as black and white as a situation can be—you flew where you were ordered, with no opportunity to pass judgment on the wisdom or probity of the mission.

Some of the guys in our unit referred to our flights over the Trail as "Beating the Tail." The Laotians had an old saying: "You cannot kill a snake by beating on its tail." Hanoi and Haiphong were the head, while the Ho Chi Minh Trail was the long, winding tail. We whipped the tail as hard as we could, knowing that while we might die in the process, the snake would survive.

Everything centered on trucks. In the air war over the Trail, enemy soldiers weren't being killed or captured in any significant number; the U.S. or South Vietnamese flag wasn't being hoisted over conquered or occupied territory. Instead, hundreds of trucks were dying a sudden death, far from their birthplace in China or Russia. How bad a licking the tail was getting was measured mostly by the number of trucks destroyed. While porters and bicycles carried some supplies for the North Vietnamese, the vast majority of materiel was transported in trucks.

Early in the war, the North Vietnamese had learned to move mostly at night; during the day, it was too easy to be seen and more difficult to hide. Nighttime was the main travel time along the Ho Chi Minh Trail; the trucks moved without headlights, with the same drivers repeatedly covering the same route for months on end. Driving in the dark became second nature for the men who lived on the Trail. Our mission was to find and destroy these trucks and prevent their supplies from reaching the communists in South Vietnam.

Making things more difficult, the Ho Chi Minh Trail wasn't a single road; but a vast network of roads, paths, and streams passing through Steel Tiger. There were dozens of branch roads, cutoffs, bypasses, and exits, as the Trail extended hundreds of miles from North Vietnam, down the panhandle, and into Cambodia. Even today, the Laotian panhandle is a wild place, a land of triple canopy jungle and limestone karst that seems to smother the earth. During the war, very little of the land had been cleared for cultivation; this was some of the most rugged terrain in all of Southeast Asia.

In the daytime from the backseat of an F-4, the area looked like a large green blanket, marked with sinuous rivers and punctuated by jagged peaks that extended as high as eight thousand feet. At night, even the blur of green was gone. There were no lights, no sign of life; nothing but blackness.

Mu Gia Pass, Ban Karai Pass, and Ban Raving Pass are names familiar to anyone who flew fighters in Southeast Asia. These were well-defended choke points that had been bombed repeatedly since back in 1965. As the war dragged on, the number of AAA sites continued to grow; by the time of my tour, the North Vietnamese had added Surface-to-Air Missiles (SAMs) on their side of the passes.

The first time I flew to Mu Gia, I told my frontseater that I felt like I had been to the moon. Mu Gia was as close to a lunar landscape as you'll find on this planet: bomb craters lying on top of other craters, with filaments of newly built roads meandering through the pocked landscape. The area had repeatedly been struck by B-52 bombers early in the war and there were no trees, no buildings, no sign of life; nothing remained but holes in the brown earth.

There was no more effective truck killer during the Vietnam War than the AC-130 Spectre gunship. The Spectre was one of a series of transport planes loaded up with guns and detection gear and used to support troops in contact with the enemy as well as destroying trucks. The AC-47 and the AC-119 preceded the AC-130, but by the end of the war, the Spectre was the king of the darkness, the most effective aircraft available for nighttime interdiction.

Fast moving fighters, such as the F-4, operating on their own, were nowhere near as effective as gunships; they flew too high, moved too quickly, and saw too little. The main job of the F-4 was flak-suppression, stopping the AAA on the ground that was shooting at the gunship. When our squadron flew at night, we flew as an escort for the Spectre gunship.

The Spectre was equipped with a scope that intensified the available light from the moon and the stars and lit up the night. An infrared system could detect hot objects, such as truck engines, on the ground. For dealing with those trucks, a fully loaded gunship carried a deadly arsenal. The left side of the plane featured two 20 mm Gatling guns, a 40 mm Bofors cannon, and a huge 105 mm howitzer. To top it all off, the Spectre had a computer that linked the sensors and the ordnance together, eliminating much of the guesswork.

Aided by these sophisticated sensors, the gunship would locate targets on the Trail, orbit in a left turn, and fire at the vehicles on the ground. On a lucky night, the Spectre might find a convoy of trucks, knock out the first and last vehicle to prevent escape, and proceed to destroy the entire group.

The mood around the barracks changed during night flying. The trucks on the Ho Chi Minh Trail traveled throughout the night, often hitting a peak just before dawn. The gunships and their escorts followed the same schedule. During the day, the lights in the hootch were kept low; windows were blacked out; the maids cut back on cleaning and laundry; anyone up and about learned to tread softly. Since the night missions were much longer than the day sorties, the life of a fighter squadron was reduced to eating, sleeping, and flying, with little free time. I usually tried to get a sortie in the early evening so I could get to bed around midnight and still be able to go to work at the dispensary the next day.

Our wing usually flew two-ship missions that took off at the same time. Once we linked up with the gunship over the target on the Trail, one of the Phantoms would almost immediately head to a tanker track over Thailand for air-to-air refueling. When the first plane returned to the target, the second F-4 would leave to hit the tanker. This pattern was repeated multiple times, with two or sometimes three air-to-air refuelings being the norm. The idea was to always have a fighter escort on station to protect the gunship.

Since all the aircraft flew blacked out, I quickly learned that the darkest spot in the world is over the Ho Chi Minh Trail at night. The Spectre had a small, shielded rotating beacon on the top that we could see but which was invisible to the people on the ground. The gunship orbited high above the target in a pylon turn, going around two hundred miles per hour. We flew about six thousand feet above the Spectre, trying to stay to the right and back of the gunship, ready to roll in on a target. If the Spectre encountered AAA, it would move off the target and clear the fighter in on the guns. The F-4s usually carried cluster bomb units (CBUs) that were very effective against AAA.

During the Vietnam War, the tactics used by gunships and their fighter escorts changed over time. The number of fighter planes, the use of flares, and the type of ordnance varied as both sides adapted and tried to gain an advantage.

Whoever designed the F-4 Phantom did a poor job on the ergonomics. In an F-4, you were solidly anchored in the cockpit by an assortment of hoses, wires, belts, and harnesses. Calf garters held your lower extremities snugly to prevent them from flailing about during an ejection. You could barely move your legs at all, and couldn't even dream about crossing them. Things were tolerable for a quick day mission over the Trail—something that rarely exceeded an hour and a half—but after four hours or more in the backseat on a night mission, I felt as if someone would need to pry me out when we landed. As the mission dragged on, you'd scoot about on your seat, squirming to find a comfortable spot, trying to ignore your sore rear end while remaining focused on your job.

The INS, which was the main navigation system we used to link up with the gunship, could sometimes be a mile or two off, so after about thirty minutes in the air, I always tried to crosscheck the TACAN range and bearing heading. This usually meant unfolding and checking my maps, always a struggle in the dark—the lights in the cockpit were kept dim to stay dark-adapted. The only light available was a small bulb on a gooseneck arm that illuminated a small field of vision, only a few inches of a huge map.

Spatial disorientation was a big threat at night. The pilot had to divide his attention between the target on the ground, the bombsight, and his cockpit instruments. When he rolled in on a target, I would call out the altitude and dive angle as we headed into a dark abyss with no visual reference point.

Making this more dangerous was the mountainous terrain of the Ho Chi Minh Trail. . We always briefed staying well above the highest peak in the neighborhood, and I would repeatedly check the map to find the highest elevation nearest our target. We often heard that the maps of Laos had been made by the French decades ago and weren't completely accurate. I don't know if that was true or not, but just the rumor of error was enough to concern me.

I almost always came back from a day mission in an F-4 excited. There was a spring in my step as I dropped my gear off and de-briefed. I had had the great thrill of tagging along in combat in the world's best fighter aircraft. Night missions were different. After a night mission, I was just glad to have found my way home in the dark. I was exhausted, mentally and physically. I had no room for a sense of satisfaction. I wanted nothing more in life than a couple of beers and a soft bed.

It was a dark and dangerous world at night over the Ho Chi Minh Trail. Our wing lost several planes during my tour on night missions. I could only admire the men in my squadron who rose to the challenge.

THIRTEEN

PRISONERS OF WAR

February 18, 2014

GEORGE ROBERT HALL—MY friend, neighbor, and hero—died to-day. He lived a full eighty-three years, seven and a half of which were spent in the prisons of North Vietnam.

On September 27, 1965, Hall's RF-101 was shot down near Ha-noi. At the time, George Robert was based at Okinawa Air Base, but had been sent on temporary duty (TDY) to Udorn Royal Thai Air Base in Thailand. In one of those cruel twists of fate, he had finished his TDY assignment but was held over to fly a few more missions.

The Rolling Thunder Air Campaign had been going on for around six months. The idea was to gradually increase the bomb-ing of North Vietnam until Ho Chi Minh came to his senses and decided to negotiate an end to the war. Rather than use the full might of American air power, as his military advisors recom-mended, President Johnson put in place heavy-handed restrictions at the very beginning of the campaign. Obvious targets like North

Vietnamese airfields and ports were left untouched. The military had little voice in the tactics used. Lyndon Johnson and his Secretary of Defense Robert McNamara selected the time and the targets—a task for which they proved to be ill-suited.

Once the target had been selected, a strike package of fighter-bombers would run a gauntlet of AAA and SAMs to hit the target, all the while watching for Russian-made MiG fighters.

After the targets were struck, it was essential to know the extent of the damage. Was it "mission accomplished," or did the fighters need to come back another day? To answer that question, an unarmed jet aircraft with no fighter escort and little chance of search and rescue would fly straight and level over the targets and take photos of the bomb damage. It is difficult to imagine a more dangerous mission.

Hall was part of a two-ship photoreconnaissance mission tasked with assessing the damage to two bridges south of Hanoi that had been struck earlier in the day. Flying just two hundred feet off the ground at nearly six hundred miles an hour, his aircraft was hit by ground fire. Hall was just three minutes from the South China Sea. Since the U.S. Navy owned the South China Sea, he very likely would have been rescued if he could have made it there before ejecting. Unfortunately, Hall's aircraft broke in half; he pulled the handle on his ejection seat, blacked out, and came to on the ground surrounded by North Vietnamese.

Thus began a seven and a half year ordeal of torture and deprivation. Hall was initially listed as Missing in Action (MIA), as is the case except in very clear-cut incidences of capture or death. His wingman had seen a chute, but wasn't sure if it was Hall's or the drag chute from the plane. Most of Hall's squadron mates thought he was dead. Sixteen months passed before his family learned that he was a Prisoner of War (POW). It would be another three and a half years before they received their first letter from him.

The early years in prison were the worst. Hall was beaten and starved, losing nearly sixty pounds. Two meals of weak broth and three cigarettes was the North Vietnamese idea of a daily ration. Looking back, this should come as no surprise; the North Vietnamese had a long history of treating their prisoners brutally. Less than a third of the French troops captured during the First Indochina War survived captivity.

The POWs, mostly Air Force, Navy, and Marine officers, were an intelligent, resourceful, imaginative group that followed a strict code of conduct that required you to resist by all means available and to disclose as little information as possible. This code of conduct was deadly serious business that I was exposed to often in my Air Force career. We studied the POW experience and our obligations under the code of conduct both at flight surgeon school and at JSS. I was even tested on the code of conduct at Da Nang before I was allowed to fly in combat.

In the Vietnam War, most of the POWs were well-educated, highly motivated volunteers who, by and large, performed honorably in captivity. The POWs had an elaborate command structure with the officer in charge based on the rank at the time of capture. A creative tap code was used to communicate with other prisoners. Today, most of the POWs cite good leadership and the ability to communicate as having been essential factors in their survival.

As the war progressed, conditions did improve for the POWs, thanks in part to pressure from the Nixon administration and the National League of Families of Prisoners of War (later called the National League of Families of American Prisoners and Missing in Southeast Asia). Letters and packages began to be permitted on a limited basis. The POWs conducted classes to stay mentally sharp (Hall taught French to other POWs) and tried as much as possible to stay physically fit, a difficult task when most of your day is spent in a prison cell.

Sometimes I was forced to confront the possibility of becoming a POW. Midway through my tour at Da Nang, I got a call at the dispensary to report to wing headquarters for a mandatory briefing. We were all herded into a room, the doors were locked, and security guards were posted outside. We were briefed on a secret ink technique used to send messages on letters and packages arriving and leaving the POW camps. It seemed like a scene from a bad James Bond movie. I listened carefully and hoped I'd never need to use the information. The POWs were men we all admired, but I didn't want to join them.

In a fighter squadron, little time is spent talking about the bad things that might happen. The threat of becoming a POW was real, but the men who flew every day accepted the risk as part of their job. Between Christmas and New Year's of 1971, our wing was sent over North Vietnam, but this was the exception during my tour—most of our missions were over the Ho Chi Minh Trail in Laos. We knew that Search and Rescue (SAR) prospects were much better over the Trail than in the North. If you were shot down, you had a good chance of being picked up in Laos. If you were captured, your chances of surviving and becoming a POW were greater in North Vietnam. Not many airmen captured in Laos became POWs; few survived to come home.

When the first group of POWs came home in early 1973, it was one of the great days of my life. Their fate was always in the back of my mind, and many in the United States felt the same way. By war's end, the POW/MIA issue had been at forefront of American society for several years. We flew the POW/MIA flag. People with different beliefs about the war wore bracelets with the name of a POW, the bracelets were a bandage for a divided nation. Most Americans wanted our POWs returned, as well as a full accounting of the MIA.

In wartime, the role of the hero usually falls to the fighter aces, the men who shot down five or more enemy aircraft. In Vietnam, it wasn't until 1972, late in the conflict, that America had its first ace. In an unpopular war, the POWs became our rallying point, the focus of our celebration. They were given the honor and respect they deserved.

George Robert Hall once compared the POW experience to the challenge of flying: hours and hours of boredom mixed with moments of sheer terror. The terror as a POW may have been episodic, but the pain and loneliness, as well as the boredom, were a near constant. The POWs devised any number of strategies to cope with the monotony of prison life.

One way Hall passed his better days was by "playing golf." Part of a family of notable golfers, George Robert was captain of the U.S. Naval Academy golf team. He grew up in Hattiesburg, Mississippi, and spent much of his time on the links at the Hattiesburg Country Club. George Robert had played all over the world, but the eighteen holes in Hattiesburg were his home course; he knew every inch of the links. As he described in his memoir *Commitment to Honor*, golf provided a momentary mental escape from life in a prison camp.

Each day, Hall would mentally leave his prison cell in North Vietnam and arrive at the country club, always taking time to greet his fellow golfers by name. These men were his lifelong buddies; sometimes he would decide to join them for lunch, and on other occasions he would visit a bit with the golf pros before hitting the links.

At the make-believe first tee, Hall would swing a stick that he had sneaked past the guards, knocking the imaginary ball a full two hundred and forty yards down the middle of the fairway. He would then walk a brisk two hundred and forty steps in his cell before hitting his second shot. Maybe it was the spot for a seven iron, perhaps a wedge was called for. Hall knew the layout well, he always chose the correct club, his swing was flawless, and he never lost a ball.

And so it went. Nine holes in the morning, nine holes in the afternoon. The conditions were perfect: there was no grass that needed mowing, no children to pick up, and he never missed a day because of rain.

George Robert Hall, a scratch golfer in real life, was as steady as they come. He never had the pleasure of a birdie or the frustration of a bogie while in prison. Every single round he shot was even par.

George Robert Hall was a genuine hero to the people of Hattiesburg, who knew him simply as "George Robert." I first met him in the early 1980s when he finished his Air Force career and returned to Hattiesburg to work. It took a long time for me to call him anything other than "Colonel Hall."

We sometimes talked about flying in Vietnam, but I was careful not to go where I didn't belong. Anyone who has flown fighters in wartime shares a certain bond based on respect, but I knew I had no license to probe into that dark period of his life.

When the issue of POWs came up, George Robert was very precise about the length of his captivity. If someone said he was in prison for around five years, he would correct them: it was seven and a half years. If the issue of POWs came up at all, it was usually when George Robert was praising one of his fellow prisoners. He held Everett Alvarez, one of the first POWs, in particularly high esteem.

George Robert Hall once wrote that, throughout his life, he had attempted to be honorable, polite, truthful, and fair. I think he achieved his goals.

And I think the same can be said for almost all the American POWs.

FOURTEEN

I CORPS MEDICAL SOCIETY

1971–1972

WHEN THE U.S. military divided the country of South Vietnam into four regions—or corps, as they were called—someone made the decision to use Roman numerals to designate each zone. As a result, there was I Corps in the north, II Corps next, then III Corps, and finally IV Corps in the Mekong Delta area of the south. (These last three corps were known as "Two," "Three," and "Four" corps, but I Corps was always pronounced "eye" corps.)

Da Nang was in I Corps—the region closest to the DMZ.

Approximately every three months, as many physicians as possible would gather at China Beach for the I Corps Medical Society meeting. Even though the U.S. ground troops were being gradually withdrawn from Vietnam, I Corps still had a heavy medical presence. These were men from the Air Force, Army, Navy, and Marines, plus a few civilians. Our society included specialists from the field hospitals, battalion surgeons, general medical officers, and flight surgeons; any physician was welcome to attend. Few of the physicians were career types; most were like me, serving their two to four years of active duty, waiting to go back to the U.S. for further training or private practice.

Each time we all met, it was like a homecoming. You saw people you knew from medical school, internship, flight surgeon school, or from a previous military assignment. The medical world is different from the military world. These folks spoke your language; the conversation revolved around medical issues, rather than military ones. No one stood on formality, there was no saluting—it was like being back in the real world.

For much of the war, China Beach (along with Vung Tau in the South) was an in-country rest and recuperation (R & R) center. After serving ninety days in-country, military personnel were eligible for three days of in-country R & R. For the troops in the bush, China Beach was like heaven, a welcome respite from the unpleasantness of war. After spending weeks in the field, the soldier got a clean bed, decent food, swimming, surfing, and plenty of time to drink beer. The beachfront was nearly a mile long, and the center was able to host over two hundred people at a time, usually enlisted men.

When I arrived at Da Nang in April 1971, the withdrawal of American ground troops was well underway, and by the fall of that same year, most of the combat infantrymen and Marines were gone. As a result, China Beach had faded a bit; it had a bare-bones glamour, just an old beach house with a decent restaurant remained. The beaches and the waters of the South China Sea were a marked improvement over the dirt, heat, and noise of Da Nang, but China Beach was nothing like it appeared in the television series from the late 1980s. The place had seen better days.

At our society meetings everyone would first gather for a nice meal, often prawns. The very large prawns of Vietnam had a thick, fibrous texture with little flavor, but compared to the usual mess hall cuisine, they were a delicious treat. One of the members would give a presentation about a pertinent medical topic, followed by case presentations. It was a lot like the grand rounds we had all experienced as medical students and residents.

After the medical program was finished, the waitresses would bring the checks. This was back in the days when drug companies would often sponsor medical education, treating physicians to lavish meals and accommodations while promoting their new drugs. Sadly, this cherished custom never quite made it to Vietnam. Inevitably, someone would go on the PA system and announce, "Is there a drug representative in the house, please report to China Beach stat." We would all laugh and bemoan the fact that with no generous drug rep in sight to pick up the tab, we had to pay for our own meals. I think that physicians, more than anyone else in the military, were able to find that touch of irony that often puts the war in perspective.

As the evening progressed, the I Corps Medical Society inevitably transitioned into the I Corps Drinking Society. Drinking beer while discussing medical topics seemed to somehow legitimize the drink. Everyone would talk about where they were going to go and what they were going to do when they left Vietnam. We'd compare our present jobs and working conditions, lament the lack of equipment and facilities, and denounce the many senseless military regulations. Most everyone was anxious to leave Vietnam and move on to the next phase in our lives.

At this point, it would be late in the evening and we would have all finished several rounds of drinks. It was now time to curse the unfairness of it all. Our classmates had finished training and would soon be making big bucks, we moaned ("big bucks" was anything greater than our present salary), all while we slaved away in Southeast Asia.

But then the sad reality of the war would intrude when one of the surgeons described some of the terrible battle injuries he had taken care of during his tour: the amputees, the head wounds, and such. We would all realize how very fortunate we were to serve as physicians. Everyone in Vietnam was exposed to some risk, but it fell disproportionately. We were bitching and moaning at an R & R center, a place many servicemen would have been delighted to visit. Compared to the grunts in the field, we were truly blessed. We all knew that fortune sometimes smiles on those who least deserve it.

Before it got too late to travel from China Beach through the city and back to base without being robbed, harassed, or shot, we would squeeze into somebody's truck and head out, refreshed by the opportunity to escape for one evening back into the world of medicine.

FIFTEEN

THE RESCUE OF COVEY 219

March 3, 1972

AT TIMES, THE USAF can seem like a small world. You never know when or where you might run in to someone you knew from a previous assignment. Reunions can occur at the most unexpected places.

I was at squadron headquarters one day when the word came in that an OV-10 pilot from the 20th Tactical Air Support Squadron (TASS) who had been shot down over the Ho Chi Minh Trail and picked up in a daring rescue was returning to Da Nang. A successful rescue was always a time of great celebration; anyone not flying would head to the flight line to welcome home both the downed pilot and the SAR team that had risked their lives to save another comrade. These downed airmen were blessed; they had received all the gifts that life and luck could bestow. They were living proof that the Air Force would spare no risk to save someone who had been shot down.

The aircraft landed, taxied, and parked, and Captain Mahlon Long, an old acquaintance from my Florida days, emerged. Long looked no worse for wear, despite having spent a full afternoon escaping and evading communist troops on the Trail before being hoisted out of the jungle at dusk by a rescue helicopter (and subsequently passing one of the best nights of his life at the bar of an Officer's Club in Thailand).

Long and I had both served with the 603rd Special Operations Squadron (SOS), an A-37 unit at Hurlburt Field. He was part of a squadron that generously took me in and introduced me to the world of flying. As so often happens in the military, Long went one way, becoming an OV-10 pilot, and I went another way, ending up as a flight surgeon with an F-4 squadron. We both left Florida within a month or two of each other, and we both eventually ended up at Da Nang. Since our base was so large, with numerous aircraft flying a variety of missions, our paths had never crossed until the day I saw him sipping from a bottle of champagne on the tarmac at Da Nang.

The Ho Chi Minh Trail was a hornet's nest in March of 1972. The North Vietnamese were moving armor, artillery, men, and supplies down the panhandle of Laos, preparing for the Easter Offensive that they would launch within the month. Long had also been busy; the previous day, he had put in a strike of Navy A-7s that destroyed a fuel dump, creating several secondary explosions.

Long, whose call sign was Covey 219, was flying an OV-10 as a Forward Air Controller (FAC). His plane was a state-of-the-art observation and light attack twin engine turboprop aircraft. Unlike earlier FAC aircraft, the OV-10 had an armored cockpit, advanced communications, an ejection seat, and enough firepower to serve as close air support for troops in the field.

Long was flying in the middle of the day, a few thousand feet above the ground, searching for targets, when he encountered heavy anti-aircraft fire. His plane was struck and began to spin out of control. Covey 219 came up on Guard, the radio frequency used for emergency communications, with a Mayday call. He received an immediate response from King, the orbiting HC-130 aircraft responsible for coordinating all SAR operations for downed airmen. It was a brief conversation—Covey 219 had just enough time to give his approximate location before ejecting barely one hundred feet above the ground.

Had Long been flying one of the older FAC aircraft, he wouldn't have made it. Thankfully, the OV-10 was equipped with a zero-zero ejection seat. Long pulled the ejection lever, and in less than two seconds he was rocketed through his canopy and into the sky.

Covey 219's chute had barely deployed when Long landed in a tree, knocking off his helmet and sunglasses and breaking his nose. He released his parachute harness, climbed down from the tree, and began to make the best of a truly bad situation.

Long had landed in the thick of the Ho Chi Minh Trail at one of the worst times in the Vietnam War. He immediately started moving to the east, away from the enemy. After thirty minutes or so, he reached an area of dense trees and ground cover near the base of one of the karsts that ran all along the Laotian panhandle. These large, irregular limestone rock formations, often covered with jungle vegetation, are difficult to access and can be a good place to hide.

By now, Long was running on pure adrenaline. Finally concealed in the ground cover, Covey 219 pulled out his survival radio to make contact with friendly forces. Anxious to establish contact, he pulled out the antennae of his radio with such force that it pulled free of the radio. Fortunately, he, like everyone who flew in Southeast Asia, carried two radios. Long had better luck with the second radio and was able to contact another Covey FAC flying in the nearby area.

By this time, the SAR process was well underway. King launched a pair of HH-53 rescue helicopters and a flight of A1-E Skyraiders on alert from the Nakhon Phanom Royal Thai Air Base, located near the western border of Laos.

The HH-53s, better known as Super Jolly Green Giants, are the most welcome sight a downed airman will ever see. Equipped with thick armor, extra firepower, and a couple of para-rescue men (PJs), the Jollys are able to hover over the pickup site, drop a jungle penetrator, send down a PJ if you're wounded, and pull you into the sky. They work in pairs, with the "low bird" coming in for the pickup while the "high bird" hovers off to the side, acting as a decoy for ground fire, ready to come in if the low bird is shot down trying to make the rescue.

The A1-Es, better recognized by their call sign "Sandy," are a slow moving prop-driven aircraft designed near the end of World War II for use by the Navy. Their job is to secure the rescue area to allow the Jolly Green to safely pick up the downed airman. The Sandys are the perfect aircraft for an SAR mission; they are fitted with extra armor around the cockpit and carry four 20 mm cannons, plus a massive amount of other firepower. Able to fly low and slow and place ordnance accurately to within meters of a downed airman, the Sandys can loiter over a target for nearly eight hours.

The SAR process takes time; the Sandys are slow and the Jolly Greens are even slower, and the Jollys need a Sandy escort for protection when flying to the pickup site. Covey 219 knew he wasn't going anywhere without the Jollys, so he spent a long afternoon hiding and anxiously waiting for the SAR process to unfold.

Once on station, Sandy One, the lead A1-E, became the on-scene commander directing the SAR mission. The flight of Sandys made repeated low passes, under heavy ground fire, trying to determine Long's exact position. Covey 219 was able to vector the

Sandys in the right direction, making sure that they got a close mark of his location.

As darkness approached, the SAR reached a critical point. The team had pinpointed Long's location, but the area hadn't been neutralized; there was still sporadic ground fire around the downed airman. If the pickup wasn't made soon, the rescue aircraft would have to leave the area and return at daybreak. There was little chance of Covey 219 surviving the night in hostile territory. Sandy One directed Long to dig in as best he could, the A1-Es were going to cover the entire area with Cluster Bomb Units (CBUs).

With only the butt of his .38 revolver as a tool, Covey 219 dug and scraped like a man possessed, fashioning a shallow hole in the rocky soil. The Sandys dropped the shell-like CBUs, which opened in the air and released hundreds of bomblets that peppered the area with shrapnel. They followed up with a round of smoke bombs in an effort to screen the area from the enemy.

The Jolly Green low bird moved in for the pickup and told Long to pull his smoke. Because of the darkness and the lingering smoke, Covey 219 activated his flare instead of his smoke, and the low bird dropped down and hovered over a jungle clearing not far from Long's hiding spot. For Covey 219, the prop wash and the roar from the Jolly made the rescue seem like it was taking place in the middle of a hurricane.

The Jolly dropped the jungle penetrator, a large cable with three arms folded inward on the end, designed to break through the jungle canopy. Covey 219 ran to the clearing, careful to let the penetrator hit the ground to avoid a jolt of static electricity, pulled on the shoulder sling, unfolded the arms of the penetrator, sat down, and was winched into the air. Long later said the whole process was just like he had practiced in his survival school training.

The Jolly Green crew pulled Long into the chopper, patted him on the back, and handed him a parachute to put on. Long's first thought was, "Hey, I've been there and done that already." The Jolly Green lifted off, taking heavy ground fire as it worked to gain altitude and egress from the area as quickly as possible.

It had been a long afternoon for everyone involved. After an in-flight refueling, the Jolly Green crew landed at Nakhon Phanom, and the celebrations began. The SAR team had snatched another downed airman from near certain death or imprisonment. The champagne was opened; it was time to relax and celebrate.

Long wandered around the flight line, thanking his rescuers, before someone placed him in the back of an ambulance and took him to the base hospital. He was in excellent shape, delighted to have made it through the ordeal with only minor injuries.

Long was a local boy with more than nine months in country. After his plane landed upon his return to Da Nang, his squadron and many others were there to greet him. The champagne-fueled celebration was repeated a second time.

At the time, I didn't know who the rescued pilot was, but I recognized Mahlon as soon as he climbed out of his aircraft. We all wanted to hear his story; after all, a lot had happened since he took off from Da Nang the previous day. He described the incident in a calm, unflappable way, as if he were relating how his car broke down on the way to the grocery store. Everyone knew it had been a lot worse.

Covey 219 received an extensive debriefing at Da Nang and was soon off to Hawaii for his R & R.

March 2, 1972 was just one day in a long war. Captain Long flew another sixty-three combat missions before his tour ended. He went on to have a distinguished career as an Air Force officer. America's involvement in Vietnam ended around one year after the rescue of Covey 219, but during that time, another nine OV-10s from the 20th TASS were lost in combat.

Mahlon Long's story, heroic in so many ways, was a common one during the Vietnam War. Thousands of aircraft were shot down during the conflict. Many men were killed, some were taken prisoner, but the return of every downed pilot was a cherished event. I regard those times when I gathered with others on the flight line to welcome a rescued airman as some of the best days of my life.

SIXTEEN

OPERATION GOLDEN FLOW

Fall 1971–1972

I HAD BEEN at Da Nang just a few months when President Nixon announced a War on Drugs. The impetus for his declaration was the discovery of a high rate of heroin addiction among American troops serving in Vietnam. This was bad news for all concerned— an unpopular war was about to become even more unpopular.

It all began around May 1971, when two congressmen—Robert Steele, a Republican from Connecticut, and Morgan Murphy, a Democrat from Illinois—returned from an official visit to Vietnam with the claim that fifteen percent of American soldiers were heroin addicts.

This bombshell reverberated throughout the Nixon administration. All drugs were bad, but heroin was the worst of them all. The common image of the day saw heroin addicts as wasted, skid row criminals covered with needle tracks who committed heinous crimes to support their habit. Nixon was worried that a wave of freshly discharged soldiers would be shipped back to the United States and go on a crime spree to finance their drug addiction. This was trouble on two fronts: not only would public safety be jeopardized, but public support for the war would fall even further. Who could continue to back a war that was turning our young men into junkies?

Nixon was determined to fight what became known as the "GI heroin epidemic." In June 1971, the President went on television describing the scourge of drug abuse as "public enemy number one." A special agency was created to fight the problem, with funds allocated for the detection and treatment of drug abuse. This was one of the few times in the history of the war on drugs that the majority of the funding went towards treatment rather than law enforcement.

To be honest, none of us at the dispensary were shocked to hear the statistics on heroin use among soldiers. We knew that drugs and sex flourished right outside the gates to our base; you could buy pretty much anything you wanted in Vietnam for a little money. Still, we thought of it as more of an Army problem. Enlistment standards were higher for the Air Force, and even though many enlisted to avoid the draft, we were still an organization of volunteers, not conscripts.

We also knew that, when it came to eliminating drugs in this area of the world, the forces of history were against us. The United States was trying to fight a problem that the European powers had a major role in creating. We were, in essence, forced to deal with some of the detritus of British and French colonialism. The British grew opium in India in the eighteenth century and began shipping it to China against the emperor's will. They created a nation of addicts, as well as a lucrative source of income to buy the popular

Chinese goods of the day, such as silks, tea, and porcelain. The French were no better, arriving in the nineteenth century and soon establishing an opium franchise that proved highly profitable for the colonial administration. By the time the French left Indochina in 1954, opium production was well-established in the Golden Triangle region of Laos, Thailand, and Burma. By 1969, the Golden Triangle region was harvesting one thousand tons of raw opium a year.

Then, in 1970, one of the spurs to the GI heroin epidemic came about when the laboratories of the Golden Triangle began using a more sophisticated opium refinement process, one that allowed them to produce a higher grade heroin (90 percent pure or more). Production was booming, but the refined heroin still had to be moved to market in South Vietnam. Drug smuggling became a second job for many South Vietnamese officials, with customs, air force, army, police, and politicians all getting a piece of the action.

America was in a bad spot. Supposedly, these were our friends and allies, so the U.S. officials said little about the drug smuggling and did even less.

Prior to 1970, marijuana was probably the drug of choice for soldiers in Vietnam. It had always been common in Southeast Asia and was viewed as one of the pleasures of life, with none of the stigma found in the United States. Since the military leaders disliked drug use of any kind and since marijuana had a distinctive odor, was bulky to transport, and was easy to detect, the battle against marijuana had some limited success. Marijuana-detecting dog teams were used at most of the major bases and were found to be an effective deterrent.

In fact, the fight against marijuana was so effective that some felt it may have led to more heroin use. Heroin was more difficult to detect. The common way to use it in Vietnam was to smoke it, but it could also be snorted or even taken by mouth (because it was so pure, there was no need to inject it). Usually a cigarette was rolled between the fingers and thumb, emptying out some of the tobacco. Heroin was then poured into the hollowed-out cigarette and the mixture was smoked.

Vials of heroin were easy to purchase, and were readily available from the Vietnamese who worked on base, from children and teenagers who peddled them openly on the streets, and from any of the bars in town. It was difficult to travel in the city of Da Nang and not be offered drugs.

Nixon's War on Drugs started in June of 1971, but it wasn't until the autumn of that year that the fight came to Da Nang. There was no real warning. One day, we came to work at the dispensary and were told that "Operation Golden Flow" was now underway.

The concept was simple and effective. Before leaving Vietnam, all military personnel had to pass a urinalysis drug screen. If you failed it, you couldn't go on leave, you couldn't go on R & R, and you couldn't be separated from the military. In essence, you were stuck in Vietnam. We all agreed that being forced to remain in country had to be one of the greatest deterrents to drug use ever created.

The screening procedure was very accurate. The individual was identified by dog tags, ID card, and orders, and then observed urinating. The sample was checked to make sure it hadn't been diluted and then checked with two separate procedures. The positives were then confirmed with gas liquid chromatography. If you had used drugs in the previous four days or so, this screen would pick it up.

Most commonly, everyone was checked eight to ten days before their DEROS (Date of Estimated Return from Overseas). Random tests and checks of suspected individuals were also performed. In addition, there was an amnesty program that provided access to treatment without penalty. We had a general medical officer (not a flight surgeon), who probably indulged in marijuana himself, serving as the "amnesty Doc." His office was often filled with airmen looking to come clean. Nonetheless, the biggest number of positives at Da Nang were detected during mandatory DEROS testing.

Statistics for drug use in Vietnam are all over the place, but I think in general, our suspicions were correct: the Air Force performed much better than the Army. Something like four percent of the Army was positive, while slightly less than one percent of the Air Force screened positive.

Drug use was never part of the fighter squadron culture. I can say with almost absolute certainty that no one who flew fighters used illegal drugs. Living in the squadron hootch was a bit like living with your in-laws; everything you did was common knowledge and open to constructive criticism. There was no place to hide. A special effort was also made to make sure that the enlisted men who worked on the flight line were clean. On two occasions during my tour, an airman working on the Phantoms tested positive for drugs. In less than a week, the offender was shipped home with a general discharge. On the flight line, there was zero tolerance of drug use.

Alcohol, of course, was the most common drug of all. I can remember more than a few men flying hung over, but I never saw anyone fly intoxicated. Nevertheless, booze was a big part of everyday life in Vietnam for everyone, officer and enlisted man alike; a temporary bulwark against the stress and boredom of the war.

Still, even a drug abuse rate of only a few percent resulted in a large number of people needing treatment. Any treatment had to be done inpatient; there were no halfway houses. With the ready availability and low cost of heroin in Vietnam, it would have been impossible to have an effective outpatient treatment program.

Our inpatient unit wasn't so much a treatment center as it was a place for detoxification. It reminded me a lot of a prison. The unit was a long, modular wing with no windows, located in the dispensary complex. The only entrance was through a steel wire door that was kept bolted and locked. The unit contained roughly ten beds, five on each side. The patients were tended by corpsmen rather than nurses. Those who tested positive were checked in and searched thoroughly. Then they usually had a few hours of grace before the withdrawal symptoms began. The patients quickly became restless and agitated, thrashing about, complaining of nausea, muscle aches, or abdominal pains. Paranoia was the addict's constant companion. The withdrawal was brutal; the men hardly ever slept and rarely ate much. The severe symptoms seemed to go on for one to two days before gradually beginning to ease. We had none of the medications commonly used today to treat heroin addiction. We did the best we could to treat the symptoms with the drugs of that day, mainly anti-psychotics and sedatives.

My job was to check them twice a day, order their medications, and give them words of encouragement. Heroin withdrawal is hell on earth, but it's not usually life-threatening. There wasn't a great deal of prestige or reward working at a heroin detoxification unit in wartime, no one received a combat decoration.

Most of the patients were airmen twenty-five or younger who had gotten hooked in part because they were stationed in Vietnam, a place with high stress and cheap drugs. These men were in a bad place and their life was headed in the wrong direction. After they had been in the detox unit for a week or so and found negative on two separate tests, they were discharged. A few were able to return to duty; some went to a treatment program at Lackland Air Force Base in San Antonio, Texas; some may have gone to a bigger facility at Cam Ranh Bay. I never knew the final outcome; one of the principal drawbacks to military medicine at the time was that you rarely got to follow-up.

Many years later, I'm encouraged by the fact that the relapse rate

for people addicted to heroin in Vietnam was relatively low: something like five percent in the first year, much better than people
who became addicted in the U.S.

Today, heroin addiction is a growing problem found in all types
of communities across our country. Unfortunately, unlike Vietnam,
there's little chance of removing the addict from their dangerous
environment. Drug addiction, like war, has no simple, easy answers.

SEVENTEEN

FINAL MISSION

April 16, 1972

MY LAST FLIGHT in an F-4 Phantom was at the battle of An Loc in the spring of 1972.

For anyone who flies in combat their final mission is a milestone event; a red letter day that signals that the hard and dangerous work is almost done. It also means that, in a short while, you'll be gone from Southeast Asia and reunited with the people you love. At last—that elusive light at the end of the tunnel really is drawing nearer.

Normally, every effort is made to avoid scheduling a difficult target for the final mission. This is the time for a routine sortie, a safe ending to a long twelve months. There's no place for heroes on the last mission.

As my departure date drew closer, I rarely thought about my final mission. I had watched as dozens of members of my squadron celebrated their good fortune, and I knew that when my time came, the last outing would be a welcome finish to an interesting career as a part-time Phantom backseater. In the years to come, my life would be a lot safer and saner, but also a lot less exciting.

Unfortunately, there was no glorious conclusion for me. My final mission, like many of the events in wartime, happened in an unplanned way with no fanfare. It was far from routine, and I didn't know until well after the fact that this mission would be the last time I would ever fly in a fighter aircraft.

The North Vietnamese drive on An Loc was part of a three-prong attack known as the Easter Offensive, which the communists hoped would end the war. North Vietnamese troops had crossed the DMZ in the north, gaining control of Quang Tri. Other regiments attacked Kontum in the Central Highlands, hoping to push onto the sea, thereby cutting the country of South Vietnam in half. An Loc, the third goal of the Easter Offensive, was in the south, just sixty miles from Saigon; a real prize, very close to the capital city. The communists planned to make An Loc the seat of government for the liberated province.

The Easter Offensive wasn't the usual guerilla warfare that characterized much of the war. The North Vietnamese brought armor, artillery, anti-aircraft guns, and (reportedly) some of the new shoulder-held SA-7 missiles.

In early 1972, everyone at Da Nang knew something big was going on. Our unit was the only fighter wing left in South Vietnam, and we were flying around the clock. The bases in Thailand were handling a full load, and Navy aircraft coming off the carriers in the South China Sea were busy, as well. I flew more in February and March than any other time in my tour. I had actually become a wanted man; the scheduling officer would call me at the dispensary to see if I was available to fly. After scheming to get a spot on the schedule for most of my tour, I was happy to have the opportunity. In addition, Tet, the lunar new year, was always a favorite time for rocket attacks. Both on the ground and in the air, 1972 was proving to be a busy year.

Nixon was determined to counter the Easter Offensive with American airpower. By the beginning of April, extra Phantom squadrons had been deployed from bases in Asia and the U.S. to Da Nang. Housing was suddenly at a premium, and I gained a third roommate. There weren't enough revetments to shelter all the aircraft, and some were parked on the tarmac, unprotected from rocket attacks.

I've always found it strange how things work for the low man on the totem pole. Looking back at the time, I never really got the strategic big picture; I never knew how it all fit together. No one ever said, "This is the Easter Offensive. We're sending you to the battle of An Loc to teach those North Vietnamese a lesson." When it came to war strategy, I was way out of the loop; I didn't even know where the loop was located.

One morning, I went into the mission planning room at wing headquarters and found out that our two-ship fight was being sent to An Loc, well out of our usual working area. On that day, most of our squadron was fragged down south, so several two-ship flights were headed to An Loc, spaced roughly forty-five minutes apart. I had been scheduled to fly in the mid-morning, but asked to be pushed back to a later flight so I could finish up with my patients at the dispensary.

During the intelligence briefing, we learned that the South Vietnamese forces and their American advisors were surrounded by a much larger communist army. The besieged garrison in the southern part of An Loc was being supplied by air. Our strike was to be part of a steady dose of American air power from helicopters, bombers, fighters, and gunships. This sortie was different from the usual interdiction mission over the Ho Chi Minh Trail. If An Loc fell, the road to Saigon would be open to the North Vietnamese.

Early in my tour, before U.S. ground troops had been phased out, I had flown some close air support missions, assisting American ground troops who were in contact with the enemy and needed help, but these small engagements were nothing like the situation at An Loc. This battle was turning into siege warfare, with none of the hit-and-run tactics of the early Vietnam War.

When our flight arrived over An Loc, the FAC gave us a target briefing and was very careful to keep us away from any friendly forces. This wasn't hard to do, since the South Vietnamese were dug into an area not much more than a half-mile on each side. The sky over An Loc was filled with smoke and haze. Everything had an apocalyptic hue; it was obvious that this was a major battle that had been raging since long before we arrived.

The FAC marked the target with a white phosphorous rocket and cleared us for a low angle run in. On the second pass, as the frontseater released his bombs and pulled hard left off the target, I looked down and caught a glimpse of a couple of tanks lying in a helter-skelter position on one of the streets of An Loc. These North Vietnamese tanks weren't our target; they had probably been destroyed earlier in the battle. They were just the skeletal remains of some of the dozens lost at An Loc.

The glimpse of the armor was so quick and so fleeting that I asked the frontseater if he had seen the tanks. He was as surprised as I was; this was a first for both of us, and it added another dimension to the war. In over fifty combat missions, I had been shot at from time to time, but I had never seen any real evidence of enemy troops; nothing other than rice paddies, jungle, and mountains. By and large, our main mission had been to destroy inanimate objects like trucks, weapons caches, and fuel dumps. During my tour, I never saw an enemy soldier or any object that looked like it belonged in a war, other than the tanks I saw that day at An Loc.

Most of my time had been spent blowing holes in the jungle and getting Bomb Damage Assessments from a perch high above the Ho Chi Minh Trail. At An Loc, for the first time, I encountered siege-like warfare, with armor and artillery, a battle that lasted weeks rather than hours or days. This mission gave me a different perspective of the Vietnam War.

Our flight recovered and refueled at Bien Hoa Air Base, located right outside of Saigon, before returning to Da Nang. I stopped by Base Operations and was told that I was needed immediately at the dispensary. Van, the flight leader of the previous two ship mission from our squadron, had been hit and lost his landing gear. He and his backseater were forced to eject and had landed in a field just outside Bien Hoa. They were both immediately picked up by the base rescue helicopter and sent to the dispensary to be checked over.

As far as ejections go, this was one of the better ones. Van and his WSO were able to pick their spot to punch out. It sounds simple and safe, but in reality, it was a very dangerous situation. When the ejection handle is pulled, your world changes in an instant. In less than two seconds, the rear canopy is blown, the backseater is ejected, the front canopy is blown, and the pilot is ejected. It's fast and furious, much like having a rocket strapped to your rear end and being shot into the sky.

When I arrived at the dispensary I found my old friend Wendell, a flight surgeon I had known in Florida, checking the X-rays of Van's lower spine. We both suspected a vertebral fracture, a common complication from an ejection from an F-4, but we weren't sure. The findings were subtle and we weren't radiologists, so we sent him on to the hospital at Tan Son Nhut to be checked.

Later, it occurred to me that I had had a close call of sorts. I had actually been scheduled to fly as Van's backseater before I had myself pushed back to later in the day. I wondered, if I had flown with Van as originally planned, how would I have handled the ejection? There are so many "what if's" in wartime, and this was an admittedly minor one, so I kept it to myself.

Around the same time as my trip to An Loc, the formal paperwork came through, scheduling me to leave Da Nang around May 16. The date, just a couple of weeks ahead of my one year anniversary, was nothing to get excited about; it certainly wasn't my idea of what Vietnamization meant. With nearly a month to go in country and the Easter Offensive rolling along, I figured that I would have several more opportunities to fly.

A few days later, one of those unexpected golden opportunities arose, an undeserved stroke of good fortune for a man who had long ago grown tired of Vietnam. One of my patients was a C-47 pilot who flew all over Southeast Asia, ferrying people and goods from place to place. I had told him how much I had enjoyed visiting Thailand a few months back, and he generously invited me to come along the following week for a couple of days in Bangkok. It wasn't combat, but I was happy to add my name to the manifest.

In wartime, luxury comes in many forms. The two days in Bangkok were a well-appreciated respite from a war without purpose or end. I enjoyed wonderful food in a sit-down restaurant, delicious Thai beer, clean sheets, and uninterrupted sleep. The time flew by quickly.

When I arrived back at Da Nang around 5:00 PM, I headed straight to the dispensary to check my mail, one of the few pleasures I had in Vietnam.

Lying on my desk, like a gift from heaven, were orders to leave Da Nang the following morning at 9:00 AM. I was scheduled to report to the out-processing center at 6:00 AM.

With barely a half-day left in Vietnam, I was ecstatic. I experienced one of the deepest joys of my life; I was going home to my wife and family. Exhilaration is too mild a word—I felt like I had been reborn.

The next twelve hours were a blur, spent packing, running errands, and saying farewell to friends in the squadron and at the dispensary. I was too excited to sleep, anxious to board my flight home. I wished I had a way of letting my family know the good news.

My career in a fighter squadron had come to an abrupt end. I would miss my last mission hose-down, there would be no fire truck drenching me with water as we taxied home for the final time. There would be no celebratory champagne, no round of drinks at the DOOM club, no squadron party. I would be back home in the USA by the time the next DEROS party took place. Having served me well, my party suit could be retired to an honored place in my closet. I would miss the rousing farewell from the world of combat, but I had the promise of a better world to come.

Several of my squadron buddies dropped by to drink a beer and say farewell. One gave me my Gunfighter plaque, a wooden shield with the wing's logo, inscribed with my name and the number of combat missions I had flown. Normally presented at your last squadron party, it remains one of my most treasured possessions. I was glad to be able to take mine home. I knew that if you left anything behind in war, you would never see it again.

I had finished my year in Vietnam. My tour was over. I had had my last hurrah. I had survived the soulless juggernaut of war. For me, it wasn't so much an achievement; it was more like a miracle. I had come a long way in flying, but no one else had had as far to go as I did. I had seen a lot of things I'd never seen before and done a lot of things I knew I never needed to do again.

The next morning as the "Freedom Bird" lifted off the Da Nang runway, the whole plane exploded in cheers and applause.

We were headed home.

Life is composed of chapters, and I had just finished a big one. I was filled with a sense of the possible, the future lay clearer in front of me. My wife, family, and career were waiting at home.

There were no mixed emotions. Vietnam was not hard to let go of. Like most everyone on my flight back to the U.S., I was certain that Da Nang was best seen through the rearview mirror.

BACK TO VIETNAM

SOUTHEAST ASIA TODAY

EIGHTEEN

FINDING A REASON TO RETURN

March 2016

When I left Da Nang in April 1972, I was the happiest man alive, thrilled to be returning to my wife and family, looking forward to leaving the Air Force, anxious to begin a career as an ophthalmologist.

My departure—depending on your point of view—came either just in time or a bit too early. The Linebacker campaign began the week after I left Da Nang and my squadron started flying regularly over North Vietnam. The flights that I had flown over the Ho Chi Minh Trail in Laos were replaced by missions up north. I would have liked to have been a part of Linebacker, but I had done my duty; I'd finished my military career and was looking forward to becoming a civilian. My feet were firmly planted in what everyone in Vietnam knew as the "real world." The United States would continue the air war for another eight months or so, but I would only read about it in the newspaper and watch fragments of the conflict on television.

By 1973 the long war drew to a merciful end, our POWs came home, and America was glad to be done with Vietnam.

My separation from the Vietnam War was both abrupt and near total. Never in my wildest dreams did I think I would be returning to Vietnam forty-four years later to participate in an Ironman triathlon. Of course, young men in their twenties rarely think about what they'll be doing when they reach age seventy; life is too immediate, and there is no reason to look decades into the future when the present occupies every minute of your time.

Besides, how could I have imagined something that didn't exist? When I left Da Nang, no one had ever heard of a triathlon. It wasn't until 1974 that swimming, biking, and running were linked in a single event to form the modern triathlon.

During the Vietnam War era, the fitness boom was in its infancy and the public was just beginning to view exercise as an essential component of health and well-being. In those days, fitness had yet to become a business; there were few personal trainers, not many yoga studios, and no Pilates parlors. Swimming was something most people did at the beach or at the pool during the summer. Biking, with the exception of those crazy Europeans, was an activity for young kids or for those adults too poor to own a car. Foot races staged on the streets and roads were more of an oddity than a real sporting event. The triathlon craze was still many years away.

The basic idea of a triathlon is so simple that it's a wonder someone didn't think of it earlier. There is no standard distance for a triathlon, but all of the events follow the same format: swim, bike, and run. The clock starts at the beginning of the swim, continues through the bike segment, and stops at the end of the run. The sport requires basic skills in all three disciplines, as well as the ability to transition quickly from one activity to the next.

Far and away the best known triathlon is the Ironman triathlon, created in Hawaii in 1978. U.S. Navy Commander John Collins, looking for the ultimate challenge for endurance athletes, came up with the idea of combining the three long-distance competitions held annually on the island of Oahu into one event. The Waikiki Roughwater Swim, the Around Oahu Bike Race, and the Honolulu Marathon were joined into a single competition. The result was a preposterous 2.4 mile swim, 112 mile bike, and 26.2 mile run. By anyone's reckoning, it was a punishing mixture of events—mile after mile, with no respite from the moving clock; a daunting physical challenge.

At first, the Ironman triathlon was an oddball event, a strange meeting spot for eccentric endurance athletes—more of a sporting curiosity than an athletic contest. But it didn't stay that way for long. In 1979, a ten-page story in *Sports Illustrated* introduced the sporting public to the Ironman, and a year later the triathlon began being televised on ABC's "Wide World of Sports."

The Ironman had arrived.

Each year, interest in the Ironman triathlon grows around the world, the event has become the gold standard for endurance athletes. Initially staged once a year in Hawaii, the event proved to be so popular that it soon spread to spots around the globe. NBC took over the role of bringing the Ironman story to the world, broadcasting a ninety-minute special each year. The Ironman television special, still going strong decades later, continues to overflow with drama and pathos and is probably one of the most successful infomercials ever created. Every middle-aged man on the planet who watches that television special wants to buy in—and I was no exception.

At age sixty, I caught the Ironman bug. For most of my life, I had been a runner with little interest in swimming or biking. The Air

Force deserves the credit for getting me off the sofa and onto the roads. In flight surgeon's school, our class had to qualify in a mile-and-a-half run in the August heat of San Antonio. The first couple of miles are always the biggest challenge; once I got past the initial hurdles, adding distance was easy.

Surprisingly, I was able to keep up the habit in Vietnam. When I got to Da Nang, I mapped out a six mile route around the perimeter of the base that I ran with friends a couple of times a week. Back in civilian life, things were harder to manage. I tried to run on a regular basis, but it was often difficult with a young family and an ophthalmology resident's schedule. When I began private practice, my life became more predictable and manageable.

One day, a friend and I set the ambitious goal of finishing the Boston Marathon. I made it on the first try, and within two years was able to drop my time for the marathon to under two hours and fifty minutes. Running provided a certain structure and identity to my life; success or failure was measured in minutes and seconds. It all seemed so simple and straightforward at the time. You did the work and you reaped the rewards.

When I reached my forties, the long, gradual, inevitable descent began—that slow, annoying decline in physical performance that is documented by an unforgiving clock. At first, it's barely noticeable and easy to explain away. I was running slower because I was training less, I'd tell myself. Of course, I was training less because my pace had slowed and I now covered fewer miles in a given period of time. It was a vicious cycle: slow running resulted in a decrease in mileage; fewer miles yielded even slower running.

By the time my fifties rolled around, my running was sputtering and stalling. Some days were good, but on other days running was a bone-crushing experience. Every step seemed to be a defiance of gravity. My body had begun to betray me on a regular basis.

As my fifties passed, the chasm between what my mind wanted

and what my body could deliver grew wider. I was trapped in a body that would no longer do my bidding. Age has a way of eroding your optimism, as I realized that the best was no longer yet to come; all I had to look forward to was more of the same and worse.

Yet after decades on the road, the need to exercise had become a constant with me; it couldn't be turned off, just redirected. Triathlons seemed to be the answer; it was the new sport in town, a kinder, gentler way of staying fit. I changed my workout habits; I began swimming and biking and cut back on my running. It was a pleasant experience trying to find enough time for all three disciplines. Since I had spent very little time in the pool and didn't even own a credible bicycle, my baseline performance in both of these new activities was very low. But after a few weeks, I began to enjoy the modest improvements in my performance that come when you first start training. I found that I was spending more time exercising, yet my muscles didn't feel like they were constantly working overtime.

Along the way, I discovered some great news: in cycling, a faster time on a bicycle is actually available for purchase. If you are willing to spend a foolish amount of money on an expensive bike and other gear, you can pedal perhaps one or two miles per hour faster, all the while fostering the illusion that you are improving. You're still many miles behind the leaders, but you feel a little better about yourself. Everything in the sporting world is relative, after all. It's the same line of reasoning that allows a golfer with a twenty stroke handicap to purchase a top of the line, prohibitively expensive set of golf clubs.

My short triathlons gradually led to longer ones until, at the age of sixty, I signed up for my first Ironman triathlon in Brazil. At the time, South America seemed like an exotic destination, but my choices were limited; there were only twenty Ironman events world-wide, and most of them filled up quickly.

Ironman Brazil, a full 140.6 miles non-stop, proved to be a long day for a man in his sixties—more than fourteen hours in total. I was exhausted but euphoric when I crossed the finish line, relieved to no longer have to suffer, proud of my accomplishment, and happy to have survived.

Brazil was followed the next year by Switzerland, then South Africa. Using an Ironman triathlon as an excuse to go on a holiday was an easy habit to acquire. New Zealand was next, followed by Arizona, and a final Ironman triathlon in China. In just a few years, I had participated in six Ironman triathlons on six continents in my sixties. As you might expect, this had taken a toll on my time and my body—it was time for a break.

I used the downtime to put the whole story down on paper, writing a book about my adventures (*Against the Odds: The Adventures of a Man in His Sixties Competing in Six of the World's Toughest Triathlons Across Six Continents*). I was gratified that so many people were interested in hearing my tales, but I missed the competitions. I kept running, swimming, and biking, heading out in the morning to the pool or track almost on auto-pilot. As the years rolled along, my times became embarrassingly slow; it was hard to imagine that I would ever be able to do another Ironman triathlon.

As my sixties went speeding past like an express train, the Ironman world began to change. The World Triathlon Corporation (WTC), the parent organization of Ironman, added an Ironman 70.3 triathlon to their agenda. The distances were a 1.2 mile swim, a 56 mile bike, and a 13.1 mile run—exactly half of a full Ironman. This opened the door for the thousands of people who wanted to do an Ironman triathlon but were reluctant to sign away all their free time for months on end preparing for the full race.

The WTC had expanded its customer base and in doing so had created a farm club, funneling athletes from the 70.3 distance into the full Ironman triathlon. Since the Ironman brand was attracting overachievers with a high disposable income, there was money to be made for the WTC. A little more than a decade ago, there were just twenty or so Ironman events; today, there are close to one hundred and fifty. Entry fees have gone up, and races are now staged on all corners of the globe. (No surprise, then, that big business showed up in the form of private equity firms. The Ironman triathlon has become a cash cow as well as an athletic event.)

Times change. The Ironman triathlon once had an aura, a type of mystique not found in other events. Tackling an Ironman required a certain dedication and perseverance—as well as a good bit of luck—not needed in other competitions. It was a difficult challenge accessible to relatively few athletes. The thought went that if running a marathon is good, then finishing an Ironman had to be even better.

Today, that's no longer the case. Ironman finishers are no longer unique; every local running group or cycling club has several people who've completed an Ironman triathlon. Once a badge of who you are and what you could do, finishing an Ironman is now so commonplace that it rarely awes or inspires. Endurance events have been embraced by the masses, the chance to be exceptional is gone.

At least, that's what I told myself as I slogged away on the roads at my snail's pace, as far from being in shape for an Ironman as a man could possibly get. As depressing as the facts of physical decline are, they are still facts. I was burdened with stiff joints and weak muscles, a mere smidgen of the man I once was.

It was around this time that the Ironman 70.3 Vietnam race popped up on the screen of my computer. I was instantly interested—this brand-new event would be held in May at my old stomping grounds in Da Nang. The Vietnam War had been on my mind and in the news for the last year or two, after decades of absence. The conflict was the major event in U.S. history during the second half of the twentieth century, and every significant milestone in the war was coming up on its fiftieth anniversary remembrance. For the last couple of years I had attended my 366th Fighter Wing reunion, seeing old faces and stirring up old memories.

One day, pushed along by nostalgia, I pulled out a large stack of letters that I had written to my wife and mother during the war. And just like that, Vietnam reentered my life. I dug out my old flight records; I even found one of my flight suits. It was easy to imagine myself in the backseat of an F-4, headed out on a mission over the Ho Chi Minh Trail. After ignoring the war for most of the last forty-five years, I was ready to return to Vietnam. The Ironman 70.3 Vietnam triathlon was just the excuse I needed.

Of course, wanting to do a triathlon and being able to do a triathlon are two very different things. Over the years, I've forgotten a lot about Vietnam, but I do remember the weather at Da Nang: temperatures topping 100°F with high humidity were the norm. It's not a good place for a senior citizen who wilts in the heat.

I gave it my best shot, huffing and puffing, pushing and pulling, trying to achieve that Ironman nirvana. I found I could make the time on the swim and the bike, but the running was no longer there.

There was, however, another option. In the Ironman 70.3 triathlon, relay teams are allowed. I could do the fifty-six mile bike and leave the swimming and running to my younger teammates. It was an ignoble choice, but I'm a practical man. In your seventies, time is no longer on your side, everything is fragile, and nothing is guaranteed. I've reached the point where life is no longer full of possibilities. My choices were limited; I could either do the bike leg of the relay or I could stay at home.

I sent in my entry, happy to be heading back to Vietnam, a anxious to see the country once again.

NINETEEN

DA NANG FROM A BICYCLE

May 6, 2016

ON MY FIRST night in Vietnam in 1971, I was greeted by a Viet Cong rocket attack. By military standards, it wasn't much to be concerned about; a few rounds exploded in the middle of the night, damaging several buildings and leaving some big ugly holes in the ground. No one was killed or injured, the holes were quickly filled in, the buildings were repaired, and the war rolled on along with barely a pause.

Decades later, I still consider this unexpected, unwelcomed introduction to war as one of the worst days of my life. It wasn't so much the fear and the anxiety that came from the ground shaking explosions, the sirens, and the flares as it was the deep sense of depression that came from the realization that I had a full year ahead of me at Da Nang. If this was day one, what could I expect in the months to come? It all seemed unfair there was no grace period, no time to adapt to life in Vietnam. The war started for me the very first day I arrived in country. It was like walking in the front door to begin a new job and being punched in the gut; there was no serious damage done, nothing permanent, but you had to wonder what else lay ahead. How bad could things get?

Forty-five years later, my first day "in country" was much more tranquil, much less stressful than my first visit. I was returning to Vietnam by choice, on my own terms, anxious to visit a land where more than fifty-eight thousand Americans had died in the fight against communism. The decades have gone by quickly, and I'm at the time in my life when looking in the rearview mirror can be a true pleasure. I am curious about so many things. How will Da Nang look nearly a half-century later? The great majority of today's Vietnamese were born after the end of what they know as the "American War;" how do they really feel about the conflict? How will they react to a returning veteran?

The Da Nang Air Base of the Vietnam War is now Da Nang International Airport. The twin ten thousand foot runways look much the same as they did in 1971, but there are few other reminders of the once massive American presence.

Early in the war, the U.S. built Da Nang Air Base, turning a sleepy airfield into the world's busiest airport, the lynchpin of American airpower in Southeast Asia. For nearly eight years, F-4 Phantoms flew around the clock, providing close air support for American and South Vietnamese troops battling the Viet Cong and North Vietnamese forces. The aircraft pounded the Ho Chi Minh trail in Laos in an attempt to slow the flow of men and materiel from North Vietnam to the Viet Cong. When ordered, they even took the war up North during the Rolling Thunder and Linebacker campaigns.

Today, Da Nang is Vietnam's third busiest airport, behind Hanoi and Ho Chi Minh City. A new terminal was opened in 2010, and an even bigger one is in the works. Nowadays, Asian tourists arrive daily, headed for the beaches and golf courses of Da Nang. The passenger terminal is located on the west side of the runway at the spot where the original base operations existed during the war; the control tower stands a little further to the north and looks unchanged. While the basic layout of Da Nang International Airport is much the same as it was during the war, the atmosphere is completely different. Today, it's a quiet, ordinary airport with long intervals between takeoffs and landings; there is none of the chaos of wartime.

I landed from the south at the end of a twenty-eight hour flight from the U.S., exhausted and feeling my age but thrilled to be making the same approach that I had done many times in the past in an F-4. As my plane taxied, I scanned the area, looking for familiar landmarks. Not surprisingly, the barracks, mess hall, base exchange, wing headquarters, and dispensary were all long gone. The only familiar objects were the half-moon shaped revetments that once sheltered the Phantoms from Viet Cong rocket attacks. These immense slabs of steel and concrete, lined in neat rows, are the last remaining symbols of American air power. Virtually indestructible, the revetments stand sad and forlorn at many of the old airbases throughout the country. A few are still used to shelter aircraft, while others have been converted into storage depots.

I began my stay in Vietnam at one of the many luxury resorts that are strung out like beads on a necklace along the curving China Beach coastline. The Vietnamese have their own names for the beaches that make up what is better known to the rest of the world as China Beach. They probably resent having the name of their traditional enemy attached to one of their better known pieces of real estate, but they recognize the branding value of the China

Beach name and seem to have reluctantly accepted the more recognizable moniker.

Even though the Chinese are avid tourists and heavy investors in the country, today's Vietnamese have a certain fear and loathing of China. I can't begin to tell you how many Vietnamese have complained to me about the Chinese. They are "overbearing," "poor mannered," and "spend too much time gambling." No insult is too small, no complaint too petty. One guide told me that he hated dealing with the Chinese because they spend too much time taking selfies.

My hotel is home base for the Ironman Vietnam 70.3 triathlon, ostensibly the reason for my return to Vietnam. In reality, the race was just an excuse to come back to Da Nang. If I hadn't found this event, I would have had to think up another reason to return. I've hooked up with a couple of expatriates working in Vietnam to help share the burden of doing the Ironman. Ryszard, a native South African who manages a hotel in Da Nang, will do the swim, while Lars, a German who works for Adidas in Ho Chi Minh City, will handle the run. My task is to push a seventy-one year old body along a fifty-six mile bike course in one hundred plus degree heat.

My first full day back in Vietnam is devoted to making sure my bicycle will carry me the full fifty-six miles. Even though my body is old, my bicycle is fairly new; I need every bit of help I can get in this race, and besides, I've always considered it a crime to be saddled with an obsolete bicycle. For probably the last time in my life, I break down my bike, pack it in a case, and bring it along on the airplane. I've done this probably a dozen or more times over the years, and each effort seems a little more annoying and a lot more cumbersome than the previous one. (I tried to rent a bike in Da Nang, but there are only a few shops in town, and they haven't progressed much past mountain bikes.)

There are many challenges when you bring along your bicycle. I've always felt that traveling with a bike is awkward and unnatural, it's like taking your lawnmower or vacuum cleaner on a vacation. The case is fairly large, and transporting it to and from airports is always difficult. Vehicles are also smaller in Asia, and the SUVs and minivans seen in the U.S. are less common. Negotiating the baggage fee for a bicycle with the airlines is like entering the lottery. Sometimes you're oversized, sometimes you're overweight, sometimes both. Occasionally, the bike is free. I usually present my bike case at the airport check-in and pray for the best. Once you've completed the race, you usually need to store your bicycle while you travel about the country before picking it up the day you fly home. Most hotels are accommodating, but it's another uncertainty to deal with.

For me, the greatest challenge of all is reassembling my bike. Some people are mechanically inclined, natural-born fine-tuners who are in love with their bicycle. I am not one of them. Like most machines, a bicycle is easier to take apart than it is to put back together. By the end of the struggle, my back hurts, my neck is sore, and my arms ache as I struggle to solve the assembly puzzle in the corner of a poorly lit hotel room.

Like any jet-lagged senior citizen, I'm wide awake at 5:00 AM with plenty of time to put my bike into working condition. By mid-morning, I'm out on the streets of Da Nang, making sure my bicycle is free of problems. Is the seat height comfortable? Are the wheels true? Does it shift and brake properly? The middle of a race is no time to find out your bike's got an issue.

This city has changed in forty-five years. None of the rundown bars or shops remain; everything looks like it was built yesterday. In the old days, jeeps and military vehicles shared the roads with Vietnamese riding old bicycles or the occasional motorbike. This has all changed in the last half-century, Vietnam has become the land of motorbikes.

It's unbelievable. I've never seen so many motorbikes in my life. All of the streets are packed, there's a mad cacophony of sputtering engines. Herds of motorbikes speed about in all directions, carrying anywhere from one to four people and loaded with cargo of every size and shape. Some have large baskets of produce, others carry cages of live animals; most anything that you would normally carry in a truck is transported on a motorbike.

The citizens of Vietnam adore their motorbikes. The population of the country will soon reach one hundred million, and the number of motorbikes is close to fifty million—one motorbike for every two men, women, and children. The market is dominated by Honda, which is primarily manufactured in Vietnam; more than two-thirds of the public drives the brand. Yamaha and the Italian manufacturer Piaggio have a smaller share.

Da Nang has just a few traffic signs or signals and these seem to be generally ignored. Only tourists stop at a stop sign. Instead, the traffic flows with a certain harmony. Riders weave in and out, dodging and turning, merging seamlessly at intersections. The river of motorbikes seems to flow effortlessly down the streets. The riders are stone-faced—no one shows anger or irritation. Unlike in China or India, where motorists act as if they're getting paid by the honk, the horn is used judiciously and never with malice. The Vietnamese appear to have mastered the art of driving an overloaded bike in dense traffic while talking or texting on a cell phone.

I experienced this passion for motorbikes firsthand. As I traveled around the country, I carried multiple photocopies of some old photographs from my year at Da Nang. Some showed me working at the dispensary, some pictured me in flight gear in front of an F-4 Phantom, and a few of the pictures featured motorbikes in the background. Whenever I would show these pictures to anyone who showed the least interest in my story—guides, hotel clerks, taxi drivers, or merchants—their faces would really light up when they saw those old motorbikes. "That's a Honda '67," they'd say with glee, happy to spot what is apparently a classic motorbike. The Vietnamese reacted much like an American car lover would react if he saw a picture of a '57 Chevrolet. Many of them would ask me for a copy of the pictures. They may have been interested in my experience in Vietnam, but I think they were most impressed by the motorbikes.

With such a large number of bikes and poor safety standards, accidents are very common in Vietnam. More than twenty-five people are killed each day on a motorbike. In such a dangerous world, the government of Vietnam makes a small nod in the direction of safety. Riders are required to wear helmets, a rule generally observed at best only by the driver of the motorbike. It was very common to see one or two passengers on the back of a bike, as well as a small child standing in front of the driver on the floorboard. These extra passengers rarely wore a helmet. They were unfazed by the fact that they were breaking all known rules of traffic and common sense.

But then, the helmets used in Vietnam seem designed more for decoration than for protection. I saw a few of them for sale in shops. They're basically a thin plastic sheet, probably around a quarter inch in thickness, with very little padding, selling for around $15–20. The models worn by women have a cut-out area in the back for a ponytail. The best that can be said about the helmets is that they come in a variety of attractive colors and that they are a little better than nothing.

Women on motorbikes provide an interesting insight on Vietnamese culture. Females are just as common on bikes as are men; you see them rolling down the road in one hundred degree weather, wearing long sleeve clothes, a face mask, sunglasses, a hat and gloves—every inch of their flesh covered to protect themselves from the sun. Some even wear hoodies and long cloth garments that extend from the head down over the neck. When it comes to clothing for women on a motorbike, it seems, the more the better.

This emphasis on clothing helps protect Vietnamese women from the harmful effects of radiation, as well as reducing the respiratory effects of air pollution. But this is just part of the story; Vietnamese women aren't motivated by the fear of skin cancer or the dangers of breathing dirty air. Their biggest concern is the fear of dark skin. In Vietnam and in many Asian countries, white skin equals beauty. This love of pale flesh may date back to the days when manual labor in rice paddies resulted in dark skin. The higher classes, who worked with their minds instead of their bodies, stayed out of the sun and were admired and respected for their white skin.

This quest for white skin shows up in many different ways in Vietnam. During my trip to Southeast Asia, the sun was brutal, with the temperature usually reaching the high 90s. I ran out of sunscreen mid-way in my travels and went shopping for a replacement. What I discovered is that the concept of a sun block with a specific SPF number doesn't seem to have reached this country. I searched several stores before finding something that worked. By contrast, skin whitening creams were everywhere, I saw dozens of different brands designed to promote fair skin. It's a little ironic; while many in the affluent west seek out the sun, roasting themselves in the name of beauty, the women of Asia avoid it at all costs.

It's an interesting glimpse into Vietnamese culture that's of little concern to me. My opportunity for pale, beautiful skin ended decades ago, if it ever existed.

I eased my bicycle out into the traffic flow, dressed in my cycling gear with its fancy pants, shiny shoes, and a colorful jersey. The motorbikes that streamed past took little notice of me and my bike. Every now and then I would overtake someone, but no one would glance my way, no one would acknowledge my presence. I was just another part of the traffic circulation, another piece of the puzzle. I yelled "xin chao" (hello) to a few of the motorbikes, forcing them to look my way, occasionally generating a wry smile.

I headed down the beach road and swung left into a traffic circle with at least a hundred motorbikes, continuing on toward the airport. As I cruised along a modern four lane boulevard. I noticed there wasn't a single building remaining from my tour. After a few miles, I crossed one of the new bridges that span the Han River. In 1971, we would travel across a single bridge that was constructed by the military early in war. Today, there are four modern bridges, including one with curvy arches that is decorated to look like a dragon. Twice a week, a light show is held along the bridge and the dragon comes to life, breathing fire on cue.

In another few miles, I reached the entrance to the airport, the very same spot that was once the heavily guarded entrance to our base. I paid a toll fee of slightly less than one dollar and pedaled in. The man at the toll booth seemed indifferent to an American riding his bike onto the airport grounds. I made it from the terminal side on the west over to my old home grounds on the east side of the runway, but could go no further. The area belongs to the Vietnamese military and is restricted.

So I headed back into the motorized maelstrom of motorbikes, enjoying the scenery, searching for something I recognized, happy to be riding a bicycle that worked.

TWENTY

AT THE STARTING LINE

May 8, 2016

EVERY TIME I come to an Ironman triathlon, I know that I've shown up at the wrong place. I never feel more like an old man than I do at race time.

Wherever you go the Ironman crowd looks much the same: a group of young, lean, and fit men and women who look like they were born to swim, bike, and run; a true collection of cardiovascular badasses. It's all a little intimidating. The Ironman requires a lot of preparation and a certain commitment to fitness, and these folks have completely bought in. They have the intensity and focus of true believers; they're the kind of people who view any free time as a provocation. They probably take pleasure in their own misery, and they no doubt feel most alive when they're nearly dead.

If I'm not the oldest person at this Ironman, I'm not far from it. I'm a wizened senior citizen; one of the threadbare elderly. I've gotten a little thicker around the mid-section than I used to be; my joints are stiff and rigid, my coordination and flexibility non-existent. In spite of my feeble efforts at working out with weights, my flesh and muscles hang slack from the bone, as if they've given up all hope. I've had to battle through shoulder, hip, knee, and elbow injuries, as well as various other ailments. In the last decade, I've gone from avoiding physical therapists to practically stalking them. Today, I'm roughly one inch shorter than I was thirty years ago. The only thing that has held constant over the years is my shoe size.

Still, you'd have to be dead not to get excited about an Iron-man triathlon. Every time I show up, I'm filled with energy and hope. This race is the culmination of weeks of training, and like every participant, I'm anxious to get started. Registration is a reas-suringly familiar process: a long line of workers handing out race numbers, maps, instructions, and small bags of merchandise. Most of the goods are things you normally wouldn't bother to purchase or even keep—items like notepads, stickers, and ballpoint pens. But since they carry the Ironman name or logo, their value in-creases exponentially. And so you tuck them away, hoping you'll have a chance to use them in the future. They're small symbols of a big achievement.

A mandatory briefing thoroughly covers the race rules and course details. The entrants watch anxiously as every facet of the event is analyzed and dissected. These fine points are important for the leaders, who want to avoid a time penalty or disqualification, but my task is simple. I will try to follow the person in front of me so there's little chance of me getting off course.

The Ironman 70.3 Vietnam has more than fifteen hundred en-trants from over sixty countries. It's a diverse group of athletes from places like Singapore, Malaysia, Japan, the Philippines, Thai-land, China, and Australia. In this part of the world, the distances are vast, but it still seems like much of the Pacific has dropped in for the race. The country of Vietnam is opening itself up to the world, and the China Beach resorts of Da Nang are becoming an increasingly popular tourist destination.

Ironman is unparalleled for spreading a message of health, fitness, and overpriced merchandise. At the race expo, the selection is nearly endless—tee-shirts, water bottles, fancy bike jerseys, triathlon suits, space age-looking helmets, race belts, gels, powders, ointments, and more. There's a mountain of Ironman gear designed to help you make it through the long day. I used to eagerly load up, but after a decade of Ironman races, I have more gear than I'll ever need.

The Ironman experience is an expensive outing. Entry fees, race gear (including a high-end bicycle), hotel stays, and travel expenses push the cost into the thousands of dollars. It's well out of range for most people in developing countries, like Vietnam. Nonetheless, this is the second year for the Ironman 70.3 Vietnam, and the race organizers seem happy to have more Vietnamese entrants than the previous year.

Many of the Vietnamese athletes are expatriates, working in one of the world's fastest-growing economies. Vietnam is an inexpensive place for manufacturing high-end, low-tech goods; the country is one of the last reservoirs of cheap labor. Even though the economy is expanding at a rate of six percent or more a year, their GDP per capita is less than one half of their neighbor, China.

During my trip, I heard the expression, "Vietnam is the new China" from foreign businessmen so many times that it began to sound trite. Triathlon is a great sport, but it's a luxury most of Vietnam can't yet afford. If you travel around the country, you're much more likely to see a Vietnamese working in the rice paddies than jogging or swimming.

Surprisingly, swimming is not part of the Vietnamese culture. Despite living in a country with over two thousand miles of coastline and thousands of rivers, streams, canals, lakes, and ditches, the Vietnamese rarely learn how to swim. The possibility of drowning is real in Vietnam, water is everywhere. In the countryside, Vietnamese bathe in it and spend much of their day working around it. The threat of flash flooding is high during the monsoon season, and boats and bridges are often unreliable. Since most adults have never learned to swim, the skill doesn't get passed to the children. It even shows up in mortality statistics: drowning, not infectious diseases, is the leading cause of death in children, with at least thirty child drownings a day.

The day before the race, I meet up with my teammates Ryszard and Lars. The race organizers hooked us up with one another, and I'm very fortunate to be a part of their team. Ryszard is in his early fifties and has competed in world age-group swim competitions around the globe. Lars, in his late twenties, lives in Ho Chi Minh City, and doesn't seem a bit intimidated by the ferocious heat and humidity of Da Nang. He'll be starting the run around 10:00 AM and hopes to be done in around an hour and thirty minutes.

I promise them a fifty-six mile bike ride in around three hours, fifteen minutes. That's a modest time on the bike at best, but it is what it is. I've been riding around two hundred miles a week for the last month, all that an ancient set of heart and lungs can produce. At least cycling is the most forgiving of the three disciplines; if you get tired on a bike, you can simply pedal a little slower and you will (usually) recover. It's harder to slow down and conserve energy when you swim or run—going slow seems to hurt just as much as going fast. I'm pretty sure that so long as I stay away from a flat tire or other mechanical problems on the bike, I can finish. On the bicycle, there aren't as many ways for things to fall apart.

Purists may object to doing the Ironman 70.3 as a relay—"real" Ironmen do all three disciplines—but those purists aren't living in their eighth decade of life and they aren't waging a daily battle against physical decrepitude. Besides, my choices were limited, and

I know that doing something always feels better than doing nothing.

I had accepted this modest challenge, and I hoped I would succeed.

American music blares from industrial-sized loudspeakers as athletes wander about, making final preparations. Although the sun has barely risen, the temperature has already reached the high 80s. A drone the size of a toy truck hovers overhead, recording the whole scene for posterity.

All this activity is a call to arms, of sorts. In just a few minutes, the Ironman 70.3 Vietnam will begin. The noise and enthusiasm are a little contrived, but the anxiety is real. A long morning in the relentless heat and humidity awaits everyone in the race.

As I wait for the race to begin, I find myself experiencing many of the same emotions that I encountered nearly a half-century ago, when I flew in the backseat of an F-4 Phantom. The same anxiety and the same self-doubt that I once had before a combat mission are here for the Ironman. In both instances, as my time grew nearer, I wondered why I signed on for such a foolish endeavor. In Vietnam, my main job was medical. I could have avoided flying in a fighter and logged my flight time in a safer aircraft. Similarly, there is no reason on Earth for a man in his seventies to fly halfway around the world to ride his bicycle in one hundred degree heat.

The night before a combat mission or an Ironman triathlon is a time of fitful, uneven sleep. Much of the night is spent lying in bed, questioning your courage and sanity. A long evening of anxiety, self-pity, and despair is the best you can hope for.

In both cases—the Ironman and the war—the challenge is great, but the rewards are even greater. These are goals well worth pursuing. In combat, your fear is a response to danger, while in an Ironman triathlon, it's due to physical stress. In each case, your heart beats very fast, but for different reasons.

Thankfully, the greatest fear of all—the fear of failing your comrades—comes only in combat. You hope you can measure up to the task at hand and find the courage to do your duty, but in the Ironman triathlon, you have only yourself to be concerned with. If you fail, no one else suffers.

Still, this comparison only goes so far. I may be getting anxious before a big race, but I'm well aware of the differences between men at war and men at play.

Sports and war are closely linked in the minds of many Americans. Both endeavors emphasize courage, discipline, self-sacrifice, and a sense of duty. Images of combat are a part of how we talk about sports, with phrases such as "blitz," "ground game," "trenches," "aerial assault," and "long bomb."

While the "sports as war" metaphor is a common one, it's rarely used by people who've actually been to war. A triathlon is not warfare; it's a triathlon, nothing more, nothing less. The stakes in war are much greater than those at an athletic event. Relatively few people are killed or wounded at sporting events. There is nothing inherently brave or courageous about a successful athlete; no sacrifice is asked or offered in service to a larger goal.

When the gun sounds, my fear will pass, just as it has with every Ironman triathlon that I've ever done. I hope I do well in this race, but I know that regardless of my performance, I am more fortunate than many who served in Vietnam. I've been given forty-five full years of life that some never had. I've experienced the pleasures and challenges of work, marriage, children, and grandchildren.

I see war and life much clearer today than I've ever seen them. I'm ready to face another challenge, start another day.

TWENTY-ONE

RACE DAY

May 8, 2016

THE TRIATHLON BEGAN shortly after dawn.

This was done as an attempt to minimize the effects of the heat on the athletes. Since it rarely drops below 80 degrees in May, every bit of help was greatly appreciated. Ryszard seemed a little nervous before the swim—he's a master in the pool, but he hadn't done that many open water races. It proved to be no problem; Ryszard handled the 1.2 mile swim with ease and reached the first transition area in just over thirty minutes.

I headed out onto the bike course, anxious to see how I'd feel. Normally, you taper your training in preparation for an Ironman and are well-rested at race time, but a long plane ride and strange food can sometimes throw things out of kilter. Jet lag and foreign cuisine can be deadly for the elderly.

Thankfully, Ryszard proved to be a strong swimmer and I began the bike leg before the vast majority of the entrants. My time near the front of the race was very brief; over the next three hours I probably set a record for being passed by the most people. It was a little depressing. A few of the bikers would ease past, but most came by me so quickly that I couldn't even hope to grab onto their rear wheel.

In the Ironman, like most triathlons, drafting is not allowed. When two cyclists are close enough to one another, the bike in the rear can take advantage of reduced drag by exploiting the lead biker's slipstream. Any biker can ride a good two miles an hour or faster with the same effort when glued to the rear wheel of another biker, so the temptation to draft is always there. Nonetheless, the rules are clear: you must stay roughly three bike lengths behind the person in front of you, and when overtaking another rider you must complete the pass in fifteen seconds.

A triathlon is no place for an honor system; the rules are enforced by race officials who patrol the course on motorbikes. If you are unfortunate enough to be caught violating the rules, the race official on the back of the motorbike writes down your race number and notifies you of the infraction. You are then required to stop at a penalty tent, dismount, and wait the appropriate amount of time before continuing. The length of the penalty varies depending on the transgression, but it is usually around four minutes for the first infraction. The penalty increases for repeat offenders.

Now, I'm not a contender, but I am good at rationalizing bad behavior. If I save a few minutes by drafting, it affects no one but me. I view these violations at most as misdemeanors, the rough equivalent of holding by offensive linemen in football. It's not a question of whether or not you draft, it's a question of how discreet you are.

The course ran along the main road bordering China Beach, past the luxury resorts and public beaches, before turning west across the Son Tra Peninsula. Monkey Mountain loomed high on the right, with the statue of the Goddess of Mercy at the Linh Ung

Pagoda. This mountain was a major air control center during the war, but the pagoda and statue are recent additions.

We cross the Thuan Phuoc Bridge, the last of four bridges traversing the Han River and the only climb on the entire route. The commercial harbor and cruise ship berths lay off to the right. Da Nang, once a war-torn village, is now a major stop for the massive cruise ships that travel the Pacific. Many people were out and about on their daily activities, but they took little notice of us bikers. The Vietnamese view foreigners with a mixture of curiosity and suspicion; whether out of politeness or disdain, they seem to make a conscious effort to avoid encounters. This isn't surprising for a country that has been occupied by the Japanese, French, and Americans during the last century.

At each aid station, I came to a near complete stop to make sure that I got a full two bottles of fluids. As the day wore on the temperature continued to rise. The gauge on my odometer said 106 degrees; my seat felt seared, and my shoes were like little ovens. I felt like I'd been baked too long; I was past well-done. The last eight miles or so were directly into the wind and I began to wilt, exhausted and drained of energy.

I took solace in the fact that I would be done in just a few miles. With no run looming over me, my race was almost over. It's only a fifty-six mile bike ride, I told myself as I counted down the markers along the course. Everything is in metric in Vietnam, so fifty-six miles becomes ninety kilometers. The military forces you to think and work in the metric system, and for some strange reason, ninety kilometers seems more precise, more achievable than fifty-six miles.

As I entered the second transition area, Lars waited impatiently. I parked my bike and he was quickly gone—a young man in a hurry. I finished in around three hours and fifteen minutes, just what I expected.

For a while, I stretched and drank, trying to ward off cramping.

Ryszard told me about his swim and the two of us found a shady spot to watch as athletes dropped off their bikes and headed out on the run course. After a few beers, we wandered down to the finish line along the beach and watched the athletes arrive, exhausted and happy. I was amazed that so many people were able to handle the intense heat; a few collapse at the finish, but most seem to be in good shape.

Lars finished one hour, forty minutes after he started. We shared a few more beers, took some photos, promised to stay in touch, and headed back to our air-conditioned rooms. And just like that, the race was well and truly over.

The Ironman was a good challenge for me. I was glad to be done, happy to check that box and move on. Coming to this race was just a means to an end, an excuse to visit Vietnam. The real reason I'd come to Southeast Asia was to see the people and the country. I was anxious to get going.

TWENTY-TWO

TRAVELS AROUND DA NANG

May 2016

I HAD A few days left in Da Nang before I headed to Laos, so I decided to spend the time sightseeing and talking to the locals. Many of the triathletes were recovering from the race by basking in the sun on the sands of China Beach. While there are a lot of foreigners, you rarely see locals sunbathing. If the Vietnamese visit the beach, they come near the end of the day. I decided to take my cue from them; I'd had my quota of sunshine on race day and I wasn't interested in getting sunburned. I was more interested in what the Vietnamese remember about the war and what they think about Americans.

For someone like me, trying to get a fair idea of the thoughts and feelings of the local population, there are basically two types of Vietnamese—those who speak English and those who do not. A large number of Vietnamese, especially those working in hotels, restaurants, shops, and such, are fluent in English. Most of them learned the language in local schools and universities. Although there are currently more than twenty thousand Vietnamese studying in the United States, this is a fairly recent phenomenon. For much of its post-war history, there were relatively few opportunities for the Vietnamese to study abroad in English-speaking countries.

Nowadays, many of the Vietnamese are hard at work picking up as much English as possible, and most are glad to have the chance to practice their skills with an American. I was able to talk with a medical student in Hanoi, a shop owner in Lao Bao, children at an orphanage in Kontum, and many others along the way. Although a hundred years of colonial reign left a strong French heritage in the country, you'd never know it today. You rarely see French written or hear it spoken, English is the lingua franca for the entire world, including Vietnam. The Vietnamese are anxious to learn English; they know that it's the tongue for anyone who wants to receive a higher education or get ahead in business.

If you can't converse in English, there's also the option of asking an English-speaking Vietnamese to translate for you while you talk to a local. Using an interpreter is a little awkward, but it worked well for me on numerous occasions. Once, I had a desk clerk help me question at length an elderly cleaning woman; another time, a guide assisted me in speaking with an old fisherman working on his boat. I was happy to have these conversations; I was more likely to get an honest, unscripted answer talking with someone who rarely spoke with foreigners.

Relatively few of today's Vietnamese can actually remember the Americans. Since a good three-fourths of the population was born after the war, you would have to be in your fifties or older to have a direct memory of the conflict. For a decade or so after the war, the role of "the white man in Vietnam" was filled by the Russians. In the nineties, when diplomatic relations were established and

Americans began returning to Vietnam, they were often confused with the Russians. (Today, the Russians are sometimes known by Vietnamese merchants as "Americans with no dollars.")

All the same, everyone has a family story about the war. There are very few Vietnamese who didn't lose a parent, grandparent, uncle, or some family member during the conflict. The toll the war took on their country was staggering. Anywhere from one to three million Vietnamese were killed, depending on whose figures you believe. The truth probably lies nearer the higher figure. Around four million tons of bombs were dropped in South Vietnam, and another one million tons on the North. Some twenty million gallons of dioxin containing Agent Orange were sprayed, mostly in South Vietnam during Operation Ranch Hand, the U.S. herbicidal warfare program.

All this damage took place over a roughly eight year period, 1965–1973. The total population of North Vietnam and South Vietnam during the war was around thirty-five million, while the United States' population was around two hundred million. Our nation lost forty-seven thousand in combat and another eleven thousand to other causes. While the American losses during the war were a tragedy in any sense of the word, they were proportionally much less than those of the Vietnamese. Many people in the United States managed, both literally and figuratively, to skip the war; that wasn't possible in Vietnam.

Most of America has long forgotten—if indeed they ever knew—about the Vietnam War. In Vietnam, you couldn't forget the war even if you tried. The damage from the conflict continues today in the form of unexploded ordnance (UXO). Some fifty years down the road, there are still regular reports of farmers being killed or maimed when bombs are unearthed by accident. Ordnance turns up in cities during construction projects, in rice paddies and dikes, and along newly-built roadways. The problem is especially acute for Cluster Bomb Units (CBUs), the baseball-size bomblets that were packed in a hard shell that would open above the ground, scattering hundreds of deadly missiles over an area the size of a football field. According to some estimates, up to thirty percent of the ordnance failed to explode and remains a danger even decades later.

Likewise, the legacy of Agent Orange is one that will be with the Vietnamese and Americans both for many years to come. When something is alleged to cause harm to unborn generations and absolute proof one way or the other is difficult to establish, the problem will never be completely resolved.

Herbicidal warfare wasn't invented during the Vietnamese War. When the British battled communist insurgents in Malaysia in the 1950s, they employed defoliants. It was a good way to kill everything green and deprive the enemy in a guerilla war of cover. If the crops used by the enemy for food were also destroyed, so much the better.

The U.S. began spraying Agent Orange and other herbicides from C-123 transport planes early in the war, in a program called Operation Ranch Hand. Agent Orange, named for the color of the stripe on the barrel in which it was shipped, contained a highly toxic strain of dioxin. American scientists expressed concerns about the dioxin; some studies showed birth defects in lab animals, and by 1971 the program was discontinued.

Today, the Vietnamese government and almost all of the Vietnamese I spoke with firmly believe that the dioxin of Agent Orange is responsible for birth defects affecting thousands of children. Proof positive is sometimes hard to determine. The U.S. government hasn't acknowledged the connection between Agent Orange and birth defects, but it is helping clean up dioxin-contaminated soil. A plant has been built on the old Da Nang Air Base that heats the dioxin contaminated soil to six hundred degrees Fahrenheit, rendering it harmless. I made an effort to visit the plant while I was there, but while I'm certain the plant exists, no one I spoke with had heard of it, not even soldiers or policeman.

Today, our federal government grants compensation to American Vietnam veterans for a variety of health problems said to be associated with Agent Orange exposure. Again, direct causation is difficult to prove, but the Vietnamese aren't the only ones firmly convinced of the dangers of exposure to Agent Orange.

Even though the people of Vietnam are regularly reminded of the enduring legacy the war through UXO and Agent Orange, they are slow to point fingers. They have lived through the crime, corruption, and poverty of post-war Vietnam, and are well aware of the dismal track record of communism.

I was surprised that many Vietnamese, especially in the South, were quick to recall the crimes committed by the Viet Cong. Since this isn't taught in school and isn't part of the heroic communist saga, I was amazed at how often the issue came up. The Viet Cong killed thousands of innocent civilians with car bombs, roadside bombs, and rocket attacks. Targeted assassinations of anti-communist civilians and their families were standard policy, with some of the killings wholesale in nature.

Depending on whose numbers you believe, up to five thousand people were massacred during the month-long occupation of Hue by the Viet Cong during the Tet offensive of 1968. Some of the victims are alleged to have been buried alive. During 1972, thousands of civilians fleeing the Battle of Quang Tri on Highway 1 were gunned down by the communists. The road became known as the Highway of Terror, although you won't see that name on any of today's road signs. Add in the tens of thousands who died in the communist "re-education camps," as well as the many thousands of Boat People refugees who perished at sea fleeing the communists, and you can begin to understand why the memory of violence committed by the Viet Cong lingers in the public consciousness.

Since the winners get to write the records, you'll hear nothing publicly in Vietnam about the communists' atrocities. Under the best of circumstances, getting an honest and accurate picture of how the Vietnamese feel about the war can be a challenge. They've lived the last forty years under the thumb of communism, and they've learned that there's little to be gained by expressing a personal opinion or criticizing the government in any way.

While I am interested at looking back at the Vietnam War, that is a luxury that many Vietnamese can't afford—they're looking at today and into the future. I think they long ago accepted that the war is finished, that it's in the past and cannot be changed. The dead are in the ground and can't come back. Reliving the war isn't worth the grief.

Vietnam was and still is a poor country, and no one ever asks poor people if they want war. The Vietnamese probably want to get on with their lives, have a successful rice crop, raise their families, make a little money, and live in peace. Perhaps their Buddhist background points them toward forgiveness. More importantly, they won the war, and it's always easier for the victors to be magnanimous.

Another reason the Vietnamese are anxious to put the war behind them is the geopolitical necessity of having a good relationship with the United States. China is the traditional enemy of Vietnam. The two countries have a long history of armed conflict, most recently during a 1979 border war. Today, there is a major dispute over clashing territorial claims in the South China Sea. Both nations are communist in name, but even the brotherly, classless solidarity of communism can show strains. Vietnam and the United States need each other to counterbalance China's rising power.

My guide, a Vietnamese woman named Linh, takes me all around Da Nang as I search for places lost to forty-five years of time. There's very little left from my days in Vietnam. The roads are wide and breezy, the bridges are brand new, there's not a dirt road or pothole in sight. I recognize a few of the old temples I once visited, but little else.

Linh, a mother of two, lives in a household that includes her husband and mother. This is a little unusual in Vietnam; parents normally live with a son, but Linh's family is better able to support her mother than the family of her brother. She grew up in that lost decade after the war (1975–1985) when the country adhered to a strict, doctrinaire communism. The Vietnamese tried to create a visionary socialist state, but ended up instead with tyranny, corruption, and poverty.

Her grandfather, a North Vietnamese soldier, was killed in a U.S. bombing strike near Hanoi. His body was never recovered, even after the family enlisted the help of a fortune teller to help find the remains. In the Vietnamese tradition, the soul of a body not given proper burial and respect will not be at rest. This is a source of great anguish to Linh and her family. Ancestor worship is a central part of Vietnamese culture and is practiced in Catholic homes as well as Buddhist ones. A shrine to ancestors is a standard feature in almost all Vietnamese homes.

Linh's husband is a policeman, a good job in today's Vietnam. He and his family had to be thoroughly vetted before he got the position to make sure there were no lingering anti-communist views. Since Linh sometimes works for twelve hours a day guiding tourists, much of the childrearing duties fall on the grandmother.

Linh studied English at the local university and works hard trying to stay current on American culture, including slang and idioms. I've got little to offer Linh—I'm a pop cultural Neanderthal. If she needed to know the titles of some old songs by the Carpenters, I could probably help her, but I rarely watch movies, never go to concerts, and barely know how to operate my cell phone. I learn much more from her than she learns from me.

A trip to the Marble Mountains is a standard stop on the modern Vietnam tourist's itinerary. The mountains aren't really mountains; they're a cluster of five marble and limestone hills located just a few miles south of the Da Nang runway. Each of the craggy outcroppings is named for the natural element it's said to represent: water, wood, fire, metal, and earth.

Over the years, villages have grown up at the base of the mountains that specialize in marble sculpture. The mountains have been whittled down over the course of decades, and much of the marble used for today's carvings is imported from China. This has not slowed the tourist trade a bit. The village at the base of the Thuy Son (water) mountain has scores of stores selling intricate carvings of all types. Statues, jewelry, boxes, tables, chess sets, fountains; almost anything that can be carved from stone is found in abundance. The Buddha is represented in all sizes and shapes, while statues of the Madonna are available for those of the Catholic faith.

For veterans who served at Da Nang, Marble Mountain isn't remembered for its stone carvings; I doubt if many of those were even around during the war. Marble Mountain was better known for the airfield built at the base of the hills. Complete with a five thousand foot runway, the facility hosted Marine and Army helicopter units for most of the war. Today, there is little left of the base: a modern four lane highway cuts through the old facility, and the beachfront property has been taken over by luxury resorts. A few of the old, half-moon shaped concrete revetments are the only sign of a once massive U.S. presence.

A long climb in the heat leads to the natural caves of Thuy Son (Mountain of Water) that contain shrines to Hindu, Buddhist, and

Cham deities. I remember these caves as being off-limits during the war. The caverns were said to be laden with booby traps. We often heard stories of Marines wandering into the bowels of the mountain and never coming out. There probably was some truth to the tales; one of the chambers just a few miles from Da Nang Air Base served as a Viet Cong field hospital during the war. Today, the biggest threat to Americans comes from aggressive shop owners selling overpriced marble carvings.

Linh dropped me off at the Laotian consulate in Da Nang so that I could obtain a visa to visit Laos. If she hadn't pointed out the consulate, I never would have found it on my own. The consulate was located in a non-descript building on a side street, wedged between some drab apartments. There were no security barriers, no guards, no national flag; just the name written across the front of the building in Laotian script. The writing was a mixture of curves and curlicues that resembled a child's doodles.

Vietnamese citizens do not need a visa to visit Laos; they're both communist countries with a long common border. Thankfully, since most foreigners obtain their Laotian visa before coming to Da Nang, business was slow at the consulate. The lady behind the desk was very nice; she smiled and seemed glad to see me. It was such a contrast to the stone-faced customs officials that I saw at the Da Nang airport.

The consular official didn't speak English and I didn't speak Laotian, much less Vietnamese, so we conducted our business with gestures and short phrases.

I produced my passport, waved it in the air like a lottery ticket, and said, "Visa, visa, visa."

She smiled and replied, "Forty dollar U.S., no dong, no dong."

I hand over my passport and two twenty dollar bills and took a seat.

"No, no," she said. "Maybe soon, maybe."

I walked down the block, wandered around some shops, drank a cup of coffee, and returned around an hour later. She smiled, rubbed the thumb and index finger of her right hand together, the universal plea for money. I quickly got the message, handed over a couple of one dollar bills, and picked up my passport.

I was off to Laos in the morning.

TWENTY-THREE

HO CHI MINH TRAIL

Laos is a difficult country to visit.

This landlocked nation of less than seven million people is located in the heart of the Indochinese peninsula. Most tourists who venture into Laos fly into the capital city of Vientiane and visit the temples, markets, and museums before heading north to the ancient city of Luang Prabang, looking to take in its rich Buddhist heritage. A few continue on to the Plain of Jars, an area containing thousands of stone jars dating back to prehistoric times. The young backpacking crowd gravitates to Vang Vieng, a spot known for beer, drugs, and adventure tourism.

All of these attractions are found in the northern part of Laos, an area we knew during the war as the Barrel Roll. My interests lay in the southern part of the country: the Laotian panhandle, the heart of the Ho Chi Minh Trail, the region we called Steel Tiger. Most of the combat missions I flew during the war were over the Trail, a sparsely populated area of triple canopy jungle, rugged mountains, and limestone karst. I saw it many times from the air, and now, forty-five years later, I want to view the Trail from the ground.

From roughly 1965 until the U.S. withdrawal from Southeast Asia in 1973, the air war was waged over the Ho Chi Minh Trail—American fighters and bombers versus North Vietnamese and Pathet Lao anti-aircraft artillery. The goal was to reduce the supplies flowing from North Vietnam to the Viet Cong in the South. Each year, the traffic on the Trail increased and the defenses grew more formidable; the number of guns rose, as did the proficiency of the men firing them. By the end of my tour, the North Vietnamese had even begun to move Surface to Air Missiles (SAMs) onto the Trail.

Reaching the Ho Chi Minh Trail takes a little work. Laos has a long border with Vietnam—more than thirteen hundred miles—but the area is so mountainous and so primitive that there are only six border crossings.

I wanted to visit Mu Gia Pass, the principal entry point from North Vietnam onto the Trail in Laos. Mu Gia was a choke point, an ideal place to block traffic and put a dent in the supplies flowing south. B-52 bombers, carrying ten times the load of an F-4, first struck the pass in late 1965, and the air-strikes continued for nearly eight years. Six years later, when I first flew to Mu Gia, the area resembled a lunar landscape. Bomb craters pockmarked the ground and the whole area was brown and barren; there wasn't a living thing in sight. The Pass was heavily fortified with SAM sites on the North Vietnamese entrance. One border of Mu Gia had tall limestone karsts extending vertically, giving the whole area a post-apocalyptic look.

Today, Mu Gia Pass is still far removed from civilization. The region, part of a nature reserve, is remote and inaccessible. It would have taken me two days of travel each way to reach the pass. My best bet for entering the Laotian panhandle was the border crossing at Lao Bao.

On the map, it looked fairly simple. Nearly a hundred mile drive to the north along Highway 1, crossing the Hai Van Pass and skirting the ancient imperial city of Hue to Dong Ha. From there, another forty miles or so west on Highway 9 would bring me to the border.

A trip that would require barely two hours on an U.S. interstate highway ended up taking most of a day, but it proved to be one of the most interesting days of my life. This was my first time in the Vietnamese countryside in forty-five years. While I had found Da Nang to be almost totally unrecognizable, the rice paddies, farmers, and villages of rural Vietnam looked a lot like they did during the war.

My guide, Phuoc, along with our driver, Thanh, picked me up at my hotel. Phuoc grew up after the war in the countryside outside of Hue. His parents were poor farmers who had no allegiance to either side during the war; Phuoc said they were simply trying to survive in an area that had known nothing but war for generations. This was unusual—the war left few opportunities for neutrality. Most people were forced to choose sides.

Thanh, who spoke little English, bore a striking resemblance to Nguyen Cao Ky, the former South Vietnamese prime minister and flamboyant Air Force commander. Thanh seemed pleased when I commented on the resemblance; he told me that Ky is still held in good regard in the South.

We headed north out of Da Nang for about twenty miles to the Hai Van Pass. During my tour, we would usually latch onto an armed convoy and cross the Pass on our way to medcap missions in small villages. Our medical team would spend the middle of the day treating patients, winning their hearts and minds, before heading home well before dark. The nights in the countryside belonged to the Viet Cong.

Historically, the Pass has been a major barrier to armies moving between the north and central regions of Vietnam. The Pass climbs fifteen hundred feet, crossing a spur of the Annamite Range. The road ascends in a winding fashion for some twelve miles, offering a beautiful view of Da Nang Bay and the South China Sea to the east. During the war, the route was mostly unpaved dirt roads cluttered with military vehicles and large fuel tankers. Breaching the Pass has always been a tortuous journey; there are numerous curves with steep drop-offs. Since the Pass is often covered with fog, accidents are common. Roadside memorials to accident victims dot the route.

Today, many people take the Hai Van Tunnel, first opened in 2005. The four mile journey costs less than a dollar and saves an hour of time, but it misses much of the splendor and beauty of Vietnam. At the top of the pass are the ruins of an old French fort, later used by the South Vietnamese, as well as some gift shops that would interest even the most jaded traveler. The view is magnificent; you feel like you're at the top of the world, even though you've climbed less than two thousand feet.

Highway 1 going from Da Nang to Hue was one of the most dangerous routes in the South during the war. Military and supply vehicles would run in convoys at maximum speed, trying to avoid ambushes. Today, it's mostly a two-lane road notable only for the hundreds of roadside stalls selling bottles of eucalyptus oil. The supply seems endless. Each vendor has dozens of yellow bottles containing the all-purpose wonder drug. The Vietnamese use eucalyptus oil for a variety of ailments: colds and flu, headache, back pain, and toothaches. It's especially valued for treating fever in children. A dab on the forehead or chest is said to work wonders.

Eucalyptus and acacia are both non-native species that have been planted throughout the country. Eucalyptus is a versatile crop; the trees grow quickly, even in the areas denuded during the war. Giant factories (mostly run by foreign corporations) turn the trees into woodchips for export, while local farmers press the wood into oil. Today, the government encourages the planting of native hardwoods to increase biodiversity, but that's a hard sell for peasants needing a cash crop. Phuoc tells me that the hardwoods take too long to mature. The local farmer who lives day-to-day is unable to wait decades for a return investment when the rapidly growing eucalyptus is a quick sell to the paper mills.

After lunch, we leave Highway 1 and head west on Highway 9 to Lao Bao. Both of these highways are major arteries that serve a multitude of purposes. They transport innumerable pedestrians, motorbikes, carts, wagons, water buffaloes, bicycles, small trucks, and cars. The highways also serve as a convenient place to dry rice. The recently harvested crop is spread out on the asphalt, covering anywhere from a third to a full lane of the road. A woman with a broom sweeps and turns the grain, keeping the crop in a discreet pile. The approaching traffic is careful to swerve if necessary to avoid running over the rice. No one seems the least bit annoyed or angry by the rice strewn across the road—this is a normal part of life in Vietnam, as it is in much of rice-growing Asia.

Phuoc assures me that we are staying in the very best hotel in Lao Bao, a town of thirty thousand located well away from the usual tourist routes. There is little in the area to draw visitors; this is a community that survives on the border trade between two poor regions. The hotel has a couple dozen rooms, nothing that would pass for serious air-conditioning, a duty-free shop that's heavy on Scotch whiskey, and very few customers. It's the opposite end of the spectrum from the luxury hotel I stayed at on China Beach, but it seems more authentic, more Vietnamese, less Western. Phuoc and Thanh have been here before and are greeted by the staff as long-lost friends. They're off for the evening and I settle in my room, amazed that the Internet has reached this deep into Vietnam.

The dining room at the hotel is crowded that evening with twenty or thirty Vietnamese soldiers dressed in immaculate starched green uniforms. Phuoc is gone, so I talk with the one or two soldiers who speak some English. They are members of an honor guard, headed to the Laotian border the following day to officially accept the remains of Vietnamese soldiers killed during the war and to transport the remains to be interred in a military cemetery. These remains, from the 1971 Lam Son 719 campaign, were located in part thanks to modern day GPS technology. During Lam Son 719, South Vietnamese troops invaded Laos in an unsuccessful attempt to cut the Ho Chi Minh Trail. The fallen soldiers' remains are apparently both North Vietnamese and South Vietnamese troops—both are accorded proper deference.

The soldiers, mostly in their twenties, are honored to have been selected for the military escort duty. Like soldiers everywhere, these men drink heavily and talk and laugh loudly. I'm struck mainly by how young they are; they all were born well after the war ended. When I talk with them, they seem more interested in American music and movies than in the war.

It will still take many generations for the Vietnam War to truly end. Even today, there are regular reminders of the toll the conflict took on the men who fought and their families. During my trip to Vietnam, the government announced that the remains of First Lieutenant Donald Burch had been identified and would be returned to his family for burial with full military honors. Burch was twenty-four years old when, in April 1966, his F-105 was shot down over North Vietnam. Mitochondrial DNA analysis was the key to identification of the remains. Around sixteen hundred Americans are still unaccounted for, a small number compared to tens of thousands of missing citizens and soldiers of North and South Vietnam.

The next day, Phuoc, Thanh, and I pick up a fourth man before heading out to cross the border into Laos. Our new companion, a local man named Son, seems to be what could best be described as a "fixer." He lives in the area, knows everyone at the border crossing, and will make sure things go smoothly for our gang of four.

Laos is a communist country, saddled with the usual communist problems of corruption, poverty, and human rights abuses of all sizes and shapes. The Vietnamese are also communists, but seem to be doing their best to become, if not card-carrying capitalists, at least cheerleaders for capitalism. The same can't be said about their Laotian comrades. There were permits to be obtained, papers to be filled out, passports to be checked, and visas (for me) to be scrutinized. All four travelers needed to clear, as did our vehicle.

The ritual of it was hard for me to understand. Sometimes Phuoc and Son would call me over to a window and the customs official would examine my passport in great detail, leafing through the pages like they contained the meaning of life. Other times, they would tell me to stay in the car. I had the feeling that I was some kind of illegal contraband they were trying to smuggle across the border, that maybe I really didn't belong in Laos.

The whole process took about one hour, but we were finally cleared to leave Vietnam. At the Laotian checkpoint, the routine was much the same, with one exception. Phuoc told me to place two one dollar bills inside my passport before handing it to the official sitting at a desk behind a glass window. The officer, dressed in a green uniform with red epaulettes studded with stars, opened my passport and deftly slid the bills into an adjacent drawer in one smooth motion without a hint of a thank you. Just to show that he was serious, he spent several minutes examining each page before finally adding the stamp. Every time I entered or left Laos, there were two or three windows to visit. Some required a single dollar bill, some necessitated two. I followed Phuoc's instructions to the letter, impressed with the power of the American dollar bill.

Once we crossed the border, we headed thirty miles west to

the town of Tchepone. Nowadays, it's better known as Sepon or Xepon, but during the war our maps always said Tchepone. We passed houses on stilts with clapboard siding and corrugated metal roofs. Pigs, goats, and chickens wandered about, sometimes claiming the highway as their territory; banana trees seemed to grow everywhere. Large swatches of the adjacent hillsides were partially denuded as locals practiced "slash-and-burn" agriculture.

The Tchepone area was one of the key centers on the Ho Chi Minh Trail, a vital river junction and storage area. In early 1971, during operation Lam Son 719, South Vietnamese troops, supported by U.S. air power, artillery, and logistics, attempted to drive to Tchepone and cut the Trail. U.S. ground troops were prohibited by law from participating, but hundreds of sorties were flown in support of the mission, resulting in significant American air losses, especially among those who flew helicopters.

Unfortunately, Lam Son 719 didn't work out as planned. The North Vietnamese decided to stay and fight, and the South Vietnamese, after taking the town of Tchepone, had to be evacuated by air. This was an early indication that our policy of turning the war over to the South Vietnamese (Nixon's lauded Vietnamization) might not be working.

Even after the failure of Lam Son 719, the Tchepone area was frequently on our target list and remained one of the most dangerous areas on the Trail. The U.S. seemed to have an almost obsessive quest to destroy Tchepone.

And indeed, the destruction was almost total. We left the main road to visit what is known as old Tchepone. There was very little to see: An old French bank vault, around twelve feet on each side, sits on top of a small mound; nearby is the bomb-scarred wall of a Buddhist temple that locals say miraculously survived. The adjacent Sepon River bank is still pockmarked with bomb craters.

The four of us spent a couple of days driving along side roads, stopping and talking with villagers. I enjoyed wandering through a strange country, thankful for the opportunity to be a tourist in a place that rarely has any visitors.

I asked about the war, but no one seemed to remember much. It all seems to have happened many years ago. I talked with some men in their twenties who were working on a long boat used for river races. They have lived here most of their life, but their families moved to the area after the war. During my trip to Laos, I couldn't find anyone who had lived there during the war.

It had been a difficult time for the country. The Ho Chi Minh Trail was constantly struck during the war and as many Laotians as possible moved away, some even retreating to live in caves. Those Laotians who remained in the area ran the risk of being forced to work as porters for the North Vietnamese or being the victims of U.S. bombing. For the people of Laos, this was an unwanted conflict fought by foreigners their on home soil.

Today, modern Tchepone has sprung up on the west side of the Sepon River, just a few miles away from the old town. We crossed the river using a bridge built a decade after the war by the Soviets; to the south lay the remains of the original structure, destroyed by U.S. bombs during the war. There wasn't much to see in the new town: a Buddhist temple, a covered market selling shabby merchandise from Thailand, and a few roadside stalls open despite the heat of the day.

One morning, after several hours of tramping around in the heat, we stopped at a garage-like building with plastic tables and chairs scattered out front under an awning. By now, the temperature had climbed to around ninety degrees. Our group sat at a table while a couple of the adjacent tables were filled with young men working their cell phones. Ubiquitous is too mild a word for it—I'm still looking for a person in Southeast Asia who doesn't have a cell phone.

One of the stalls was a sort of beauty salon. I watched as a middle-aged woman got her hair cut and then received a manicure and a pedicure. Finally, in the ultimate quest for beauty, she had her ears cleaned. A long pair of bayonet shaped forceps was used to insert various swabs and solutions into the ear canal. It was a serious and delicate procedure—the feminine quest for beauty exists in all cultures and knows no limits.

The stall adjacent to the beauty salon was used for cooking. Large pots boiled over the flames of a propane gas cooker. Some of the men were eating a dish of noodles and pig organs. We all had a beer which was served semi-cold, ice added to the glass as needed. As time passed, our drink was freshened up and replenished.

The men all work at a nearby plant owned by some foreigners that manufactures some kind of electric device. They had nothing to say about the war; they were more interested in their smartphones. Everyone was drinking Beerlao, a rice-based lager made in Laos. Beerlao is an ordinary tasting lager that has obtained a cult-like status in much of the world, probably in part because it's hard to find anywhere other than in Laos. Beerlao did wonders. After a couple of rounds, the war seemed ages in the past. Drinking beer with ice on a hot morning and watching a lady have her ears cleaned, all while the scent of pig organs floated in the air, seemed like a much better way to pass the time.

There was really no safe place to live in Laos during the war. It wasn't just the Ho Chi Minh Trail in the panhandle that was involved in the so called "Secret War." Early in the 1960s, the CIA led a campaign to help the Royal Laotian forces in their fight against the communist troops of the Pathet Lao and the North Vietnamese. They enlisted the support of the hill tribe Hmong people and their charismatic leader Vang Pao. Then, in 1962, the Geneva Accords were signed, guaranteeing a free and neutral Laos.

A coalition government was formed, and U.S. and North Vietnamese troops were scheduled to leave Laos. Things were finally looking up for the divided country.

The North Vietnamese violated the Geneva Accords from the beginning, continuing to move troops and supplies down the Trail to South Vietnam, maintaining their support to their communist brethren, the Pathet Lao in Laos and the Viet Cong in South Vietnam. The CIA also stayed, funneling support to the Hmong fighters, while the Seventh Air Force kept bombing the Trail. The Secret War, waged in a neutral nation, continued until 1973.

Early in my Air Force career, I had an opportunity to participate in the Secret War in Laos. My first assignment after flight surgeon's school was with the 1st Special Operations Wing at Hurlburt Field, Florida, a unit that focused on unconventional warfare, including the clandestine support of the war in Laos. My squadron commander was a young major named Richard Secord.

When I arrived at Hurlburt in the fall of 1970, Secord was commander of the 603rd Special Operations Squadron, an A-37 unit employed in counter-insurgency. Knowledgeable regarding both the Middle East and Southeast Asia, he went on to hold a variety of posts before retiring as a Major General. Secord's greatest claim to fame, or notoriety, came with the Iran-Contra Affair in the 1980s, a scheme to provide funds to the Nicaraguan Contra rebels from profits gained by selling arms to Iran. Secord helped manage the covert arms sales through secret Swiss bank accounts, reportedly making a couple of million dollars in the process.

Major Secord knew a lot about the Secret War, while I knew next to nothing. I could barely find the country of Laos on a map. I had been at Hurlburt for less than a week when I was called into an office with a couple of colonels and asked if I wanted to volunteer to go to Laos to provide medical care for CIA personnel helping the Hmong fight the Pathet Laos and North Vietnamese. The colonels told me I would be "sheep-dipped," which I later learned meant that I would be a civilian assigned to the CIA, possibly using a different name.

This was an easy choice. I had just arrived in Florida and my son was two months old. Showing my true colors, I chose not to volunteer. No one seemed annoyed or upset, Major Secord appeared happy to have me on staff as a flight surgeon. My next opportunity to go to Laos came all too soon, via an F-4 just ten months later.

It would be nearly another forty-six years before I actually set foot in the country.

Fifty years later, the scars of the war in Laos are too deep to have completely healed. The landscape was devastated during the conflict. Some two million tons of ordnance was dropped on the country, making Laos the most heavily bombed nation per capita in the history of the world. Today, you see old bomb casings used as supports for houses and sheds; fuel tanks jettisoned by bombers now serve as boats; piles of different types of ordnance are used as backdrops for photo-ops for tourists. Poor farmers harvest the relics of the war to sell to scrap dealers, one of the few cash crops in the countryside.

The worst legacy of the war in Laos is the problem of the unexploded ordnance (UXO). Up to a third of the bombs dropped never exploded and continue to wreak havoc a half-century later. Particularly dangerous are the Cluster Bomb Units (CBUs), large canisters that opened in mid-air above the target scattering hundreds of small explosive bomblets over a large area. These tennis ball sized bomblets (known as "bombies" in Laos) continue to cause injury and death—particularly among children. Some twenty thousand people are estimated to have been killed or injured in Laos since the war ended. The UXO threat continues to hamper the daily life and long-term development of this nation.

The danger still lurks in the forest and fields, hindering the economy in many ways.

There are ongoing national and international efforts, supported in a small way by the U.S., to clear Laos of UXO. Most commonly, metal detectors are used to discover the ordnance, which is then marked and later detonated. This "mag and flag" technique is slow, tedious, and dangerous work. It will take many more decades to make Laos safe.

For the people of Laos, the Vietnam War still lingers. Everyone I talked to was well aware of the UXO problem and felt the U.S. should do more to help. I completely agree—I can't think of a better place to spend foreign aid dollars.

TWENTY-FOUR

HANOI

MY TIME IN Laos was done. I had set foot on the Ho Chi Minh Trail, walking the same jungle paths tread by thousands of North Vietnamese soldiers headed to the south. The damage from the war is still evident fifty years later, but the people of Laos, resilient and optimistic, are moving forward.

I headed back to Da Nang to fly to Hanoi for a couple of days on my own before joining a tour group. Phuoc, Thanh, and I took a different route back to the city, stopping at a beach resort south of Hue for lunch. (Everyone has heard of China Beach, but I never realized that there were many lovely beaches on the northern side of the Hai Van Pass.) The restaurant was packed with South Korean tourists; we had driven through a heavy rainstorm and the weather seems to have forced everyone inside. Rain never seems to fall lightly in Vietnam, the tropical downpours have an intensity like nowhere else.

After lunch, a trip through the Hai Van Tunnel put us in the outskirts of Da Nang ahead of schedule. When Phuoc dropped me at the airport, I felt like I was saying goodbye to an old friend. I had spent a lot of time with my guide and had asked him hundreds of questions; he was probably happy to rid himself of this inquisitive American senior citizen who tried to talk to everyone he saw and finally enjoy some peace and quiet with his family.

I was excited to be heading to Hanoi, the cultural and political center of the country. During my year in Vietnam, Hanoi was the most dangerous place in the world, the area where the men of Rolling Thunder ran the triple gauntlet of AAA, SAMs, and MiG aircraft, the city where most of the American POWs were held.

Rolling Thunder had ended over two years prior to my arrival in Southeast Asia. The Linebacker campaign, which sent U.S. fighters back over North Vietnam, began a week after I came home. Some have called this interval the "halftime" of the war up north, but that wasn't quite true—our wing had flown missions over North Vietnam between Christmas and New Year's in 1971. But in general, the country was mostly off-limits from the end of 1968 until May 1972.

I had always thought of Hanoi as a dark, dismal place. When you've never actually seen a city in person, your mind uses the few photos you've seen, adds in what you've read, and conjures up an image. I saw Hanoi as a city of bunkers, laced with AAA sites and SAM installations. The people wore either black pajamas or dull green uniforms with ugly pith helmets. In my mind, Hanoi was the place where the Devil went on holiday.

New York Times journalist Harrison Salisbury visited Hanoi around Christmas 1966, one of the first Americans allowed in the country. I read his book, *Behind the Lines: Hanoi* while I was in medical school. Salisbury painted a picture of devastation and destruction; his writings made the city seem like Dresden or Tokyo.

The reality was different. For much of the war, up until December 1972, Hanoi was one of the safest places in all of Vietnam. The U.S. had a thirty mile restricted zone around the city, and

Hanoi was basically off-limits to American fighters. Some bombs surely went astray—things happen when you're trying to dodge AAA and SAMs—but in general, the damage was much less than described and certainly unintentional.

Many people view the whole Vietnam War as a massive unloading of bombs over the entire country of North Vietnam. They picture giant B-52s dumping ordnance on Hanoi around the clock. There were plenty of bombs dropped on the North, but it was the nation of South Vietnam that endured the brunt of the air and ground war; around four times as many bombs were dropped in the south compared to the north. Even the small, supposedly neutral country of Laos received nearly double the ordnance that the North Vietnamese received.

At the Hanoi airport, the concrete revetments still shelter the Vietnamese fighter jets as they did fifty years ago. During much of the war, attacking the MiG fighters on the ground wasn't permitted; they had to be in the air. It was a bit like bird hunting is today; it's fine to hit the birds on the fly, but it is bad form to shoot one on the ground, sitting in a tree, or on a power line. Those were just some of the rules of engagement promulgated by Lyndon Johnson. Looking back, the rules seem bizarre and foolish, designed to kill American airmen rather than win the war.

My guide, George, sped me through the airport and downtown to my hotel. The custom of adopting an English first name for dealing with English-speaking visitors is very common in China, but I rarely saw it in Vietnam. The Vietnamese seem proud of their names and are often anxious to explain their meanings.

My hotel was near Hoan Kiem Lake, a stunningly beautiful twenty-five acre body of water surrounded by a lovely promenade. This spot was more alive than any place I saw in Vietnam. The area was full of people strolling, exercising, dancing, hawking merchandise, playing badminton, eating, or enjoying a game of chess. The city seemed to never sleep; revelers were out late at night, and merchants were on the go before dawn. If you don't like crowds, Hanoi probably isn't for you.

Immediately to the north of Hoan Kiem Lake is the Old Quarter, a warren of narrow streets and shops which has changed little in over five hundred years. Originally, each street sold a specific type of goods (herbs, silk, cotton, etc.) and the street names of today still carry those labels.

The Old Quarter is a delightful place for a morning stroll. The people of Hanoi seem oblivious to foreign tourists; the city is a popular destination for Asian as well as Western visitors. I rarely garnered a glance from any of the natives. The Vietnamese squatted in the doorways or sat on small plastic chairs, talking and eating breakfast, seemingly unaware of curious foreigners.

At the opposite end of Hoan Kiem Lake are the grand boulevards and wide pavements of the French Quarter. After the hectic, narrow streets of the Old Quarter, the elegant Parisian-style buildings of the French Quarter seemed to belong to another world. By the late nineteenth century, the French had established firm control of their colony of Indochina and began constructing elegant buildings like the Opera House and the Hotel Metropole, as well as stylish villas to house colonial officials. Today, the French heritage is preserved in the French Quarter; the spaces are greater, the architecture is lovely, and the crowds are thinner. The French never fail to impress, but their imprint on Vietnam is fading with time.

George had left me pretty well alone in Hanoi, and I had been coming and going on my own schedule. He did, however, manage to hook me into going to a water puppet show.

The last thing in the world that I wanted to do was to watch little wooden figures go through their act. It was the type of event you force your grandchildren to attend, and even then it's a poor second to video games in their eyes. A water puppet spectacle was certainly no place for a man in his seventies. If you have a finite number of days left on the planet, you don't want to waste any watching puppets.

George was persistent, so I signed on for the show. I think his persuasiveness was sincere; he was genuinely proud of this Hanoi tradition.

In the end, George did me right—the water puppets were an interesting sight to see, much better than wasting time in a bar. The show was held in a theater with comfortable seating. The stage was a waist-deep pool of water around thirteen feet long on each side. The brightly colored puppets, made out of lacquered wood, were controlled by puppeteers standing in the waist-deep water hidden behind a screen. The puppeteers maneuvered the wooden figures using long, submerged bamboo rods.

The show consisted of a series of skits based on famous Vietnamese legends and folklore. Many dealt with everyday rural life, such as the rice harvest or fishing. An orchestra of drums, bells, flutes, and strings provided the soundtrack. Everything was in Vietnamese, but the themes were universal and easy to grasp; I could quickly identify the poor maiden, the village clown, and the evil rich man.

The show once again reminded me that most must-see sights are usually must-see for a reason. It's best to leave your sophisticated ways at home and join in. I've found that some of my best experiences have come from being herded around with other tourists at local cultural shows.

Since my tour group was due in from the United States and I would soon be on a scheduled itinerary, I tried to squeeze in a visit to the Ho Chi Minh Mausoleum. I've always been fascinated at the way communist countries entomb and deify their dictators and despots. If you install an atheistic system in a country, you have to have someone for the young to worship once the old people of faith die off.

Vladimir Lenin was the first of the comrades to be embalmed and given his own mausoleum. Lenin supposedly asked to be interred, but his place in the communist pantheon was too important to let him be buried in the ground. His body is still around, having survived the collapse of the Soviet Union and the death of communism in Russia.

In North Korea, it's a family affair. Both Kim Il Sung and his son Kim Jung Il are on public display, even years after their passing. Yet it is Chairman Mao Zedong of China who takes top honors. He rests in a mausoleum that dominates the vast Tiananmen Square in Beijing. Mao's portrait is everywhere in China, including each piece of Chinese currency. When I visited his mausoleum a few years back, every single visitor seemed distraught and despondent, as if the most important person in their life had just passed away.

The Ho Chi Minh Mausoleum is located in the center of Ba Dinh Square in Hanoi, the spot where Ho proclaimed the establishment of the Democratic Republic of Vietnam on September 2, 1945. Uncle Ho, as he is commonly known, died in 1969, right in the middle of the Vietnam War. His will reportedly included instructions for the cremation of his remains, but his wishes were not to be. Ho's comrades had other ideas; it was important to keep the father of the country above ground, a symbol of the nation. In 1973, inspired by Lenin's tomb in Moscow and using marble quarried from Marble Mountain in Da Nang, the communists began work on Ho's tomb. Two years later, the mausoleum opened and the Vietnamese have been coming in droves to pay tribute ever since.

I waited in line for nearly an hour before passing through security and filing silently past the dimly lit glass case that held the great man's remains. A military honor guard stood at attention as the mostly Vietnamese crowd shuffled by in quick order; no dilly-dallying was tolerated. The Vietnamese were very respectful of their national hero, but there was little of the weeping and wailing I'd seen at Chairman Mao's mausoleum.

Uncle Ho, the father of the country, is held in highest esteem by the Vietnamese. His picture shows up around the nation on posters and banners, in shop windows, and hanging from utility poles, especially around election time. His face also graces every single piece of currency. Whenever I open my wallet, I'm greeted by Ho's goateed, half-smiling image. For most rulers, you only live once, and when you're dead you're done, but that's not the case for leaders in the communist world.

Still, it's not quite as bad as China or North Korea. Ho Chi Minh is respected, not worshipped. I was in Ho Chi Minh City on May 19, Uncle Ho's birthday, which is a public holiday. The celebration was muted; business went on as usual. The Vietnamese have seen a lot in their lifetimes, and the past is rapidly receding. They seem more interested in the future, in improving their lot, than in looking back.

I had the good fortune to link up with Vietnam Battlefield Tours for much of my trip to Southeast Asia. Vietnam Battlefield Tours is more of a labor of love for a handful of Vietnam veterans than a true business. The organization often brings along, at no charge, veterans who are unable to afford the cost of the trip. Their prices are very reasonable, and it's the only tour I've ever been on where no tipping is allowed, not even for tour guides.

Our guide, Tex, is a decorated Marine veteran who has taken groups to Southeast Asia more than forty times. One of the founders and directors of the non-profit corporation, Tex is one of the most genuine people I've ever met, a respected friend and mentor to hundreds of people who served during the war.

Many of the people Tex takes to Vietnam are veterans of the war: soldiers, Marines, and airmen looking to return to a country they were once very glad to be rid of. Some bring wives or children, eager to explain to their family what they did in a war so many years distant. A few are so old or lame that they have to be helped on and off the bus; others are eager and able to hit the ground and search for familiar sights in a changed country.

Our tour included a group of college students, several veterans, and even a couple of college professors. The emphasis was on battlefields, military museums, and other sites of interest to those who had served in the war.

Tex usually plans the itinerary to include a stop at a spot where each of the veterans served. A few want to go to a certain firebase or to a location where they were once in a fierce firefight; others want to return to an area where a buddy died in action. Sometimes, children come back to search for the spot where their father was killed.

An early stop was at the Hoa Lo Prison, better known to American POWs as the Hanoi Hilton. The building was originally built by the French in the late nineteenth century to house Vietnamese detainees, including political prisoners fighting for independence from French colonial rule.

On August 5, 1964, naval aviator Everett Alvarez, Jr., flying a strike mission after the Gulf of Tonkin incident, was shot down and became the first U.S. POW sent to Hoa Lo. Hundreds more were incarcerated between 1964 and 1973, the majority of them pilots and backseaters shot down during the Rolling Thunder campaign. The number of new POWs fell off until the bombing of North Vietnam resumed in 1972 with the Linebacker campaign.

The North Vietnamese had several prisons to house American POWs, all appropriately named by their U.S. captives. Alcatraz sheltered some of the recalcitrant Americans, Dirty Bird placed the POWs next to a power plant, and others included the Zoo, the Briarpatch, and the Plantation.

The common theme for POWs up until around 1969 was torture—rope bindings, beatings, starvation, no medical care, leg irons, and prolonged solitary confinement. Following Ho Chi Minh's death in 1969, the treatment of the POWs slowly began to improve. After U.S. forces raided the Son Tay Prison Camp in the fall of 1970, most of the POWs were moved from outlying prisons into the Hanoi Hilton.

From time to time, the North Vietnamese would bring in American anti-war activists for a visit. People like Jane Fonda or Tom Hayden would testify to the damage caused by U.S. bombing and the great treatment POWs were receiving. Fonda even found time for a photo-op sitting atop a North Vietnamese anti-aircraft gun.

Like the rest of the war, that's all history now. Most of the Hanoi Hilton was demolished and replaced by high-rise buildings. There's still a Hilton hotel in town, but it's located several blocks away and is known as the Hilton Hanoi Opera.

What is left of the original Hoa Lo Prison serves as a museum that mostly documents the Vietnamese experience under French colonialism. The entrance to the massive stone building is through an art nouveau-style arched doorway labeled "Maison Centrale"— the French big house. The prison cells were poorly-lit, poorly-ventilated rooms that sweltered in the summer and froze during the winter. The Vietnamese prisoners were kept in leg irons or in group stocks. One room holds the guillotine used by the French; gruesome photos on the wall show baskets full of heads severed by the instrument of death.

The ordeal of the Vietnamese under the French was colonialism at its brutal worst. Hoa Lo was a breeding ground, a de facto training school for Vietnamese nationalists. Many of the nation's leaders spent time at the prison.

The experience of the American POWs at Hoa Lo, by contrast, is documented mainly by old photographs. The men are shown playing basketball, singing Christmas carols, being attended to by North Vietnamese medical personnel. It seems more like a summer camp than a prison. Several signs condemn the United States for supporting the South Vietnamese and for bombing the North.

There's no mention of torture, of course. The Vietnamese to this day deny that it occurred. The reality is far different. After the war, dozens of POWs wrote memoirs about their experience in captivity. Torture is a central part of most of their stories; many considered it a fate worse than death.

One display case contains John McCain's flight suit, along with the parachute that saved him. McCain was shot down in October 1967 on his twenty-third combat mission and had the misfortune to land in Truc Bach Lake, right in the middle of Hanoi. Three of his limbs were broken during his ejection from the aircraft. He was beaten and bayonetted, and his flight suit cut away. (Senator McCain, who has visited Hoa Lo many times, maintains that the flight suit on display is not his.) We also visited a poorly-kept monument on the banks of the Truc Bach Lake that commemorates John McCain's capture.

Any Vietnamese I talked to for any length of time invariably brought up John McCain's name, as well as that of Pete Peterson. Peterson, another POW, was the first U.S. Ambassador to Vietnam. The two men are well-known, well-liked, and highly respected. In fact, there is probably no greater advocate of reconciliation between the United States and Vietnam than the senator from Arizona. McCain has led the difficult push for normalization of relations between the two countries, an effort that continues today. It's a never-ending effort to replace old grievances with new hope.

Not too far away from Truc Bach Lake is another lake (actually, more of a pond) that contains some remnants of a B-52. Huu Tiep Lake, or B-52 Lake as it is better known, contains some of the twisted wreckage of the large bomber, shot down during the Linebacker II campaign in late December 1972. A couple of tires pierce the surface; weeds grow from most of the plane's carcass. There is a plaque that describes the downing of the aircraft, but little else. The Vietnamese seem oblivious to the aircraft's presence. The lake can only be reached through a maze of streets so narrow that only pedestrians and motorbikes can enter. No one gives it a second glance; it's a relic of a war that happened a very long time ago.

It's easy, decades later when confronted by the wreckage of American planes or the horror of prison life, to resurrect a certain bitterness toward the other side. McCain and Peterson probably long ago realized that the older you get, the higher the toll that hatred takes on your existence. They elected to let the future bury the past. Their example is a good one to try to follow.

TWENTY-FIVE

TRAVELING WITH THE MARINES

OUR GROUP FLEW from Hanoi to Pleiku before beginning a week-long journey that included many of the major battle sites of the Vietnam War. With the exception of the first day in the Central Highlands, most of our time was spent in I Corps, the northern-most region of South Vietnam that abuts the DMZ.

No area of Vietnam was safe, but this was a particularly dangerous region; over half of the combat deaths during the war happened in I Corps. The U.S. Marines served in this area with great distinction; almost every Marine who died in Vietnam perished in I Corps. Although the Marines comprised just fourteen percent of the troops during the war, they suffered more than twenty-five percent of the casualties. Their story is one of bravery and heroism.

After visiting Kontum, we headed east to Qui Nhon on the coast. From there, we turned north, visiting My Lai, the site of the infamous massacre, before stopping at Quang Ngai. We continued along the coast past Chu Lai Air Base to the tourist town of Hoi An, our base for a day trip to the Champa ruins at My Son.

I retraced my steps as we traveled north to Da Nang, across the Hai Van Pass, and onto Hue. Heading northwest, we traversed the rugged A Shau Valley before reaching Khe Sanh, site of a seventy-seven day siege. We then turned back east along the strategically significant Highway 9, detouring for sites like Camp Carroll, the Rockpile, Con Thien, and Dong Ha.

I felt fortunate to be traveling with Marine veterans. The U.S. Marines first came ashore at Da Nang in early 1965 to secure the air base, and they were still there the day I left, patrolling the country around Da Nang in order to cut down on rocket attacks. Even today, it's easy to find Marines in I Corps. At most places we stopped, we ran into veterans of the Corps who had returned to tour the country. I would guess that more Marines visit Vietnam than any other branch of the military, probably because their experience was more intense, more visceral than most who served.

Our days were long and hot, and we spent much of our time hiking to the top of some former firebase or landing zone. While Tex had usually been to these spots before, the places were unmarked and had often become overgrown. An area that once held massive artillery pieces was now a mature rubber plantation, or simply a hilltop reclaimed by forty-five years of growth. Sometimes, aided by GPS, we would search for the precise spot where a Medal of Honor winner or a hometown hero had died.

Trekking in Vietnam is a challenge; the heat and humidity were unrelenting, and we would often head out in one direction only to backtrack up another path. Many times, the view from the top was obscured by decades of vegetation.

I enjoyed the hikes—they gave me some sense of the obstacles faced by the ground troops during the war. The college students saw it all as a great adventure and never once complained. I believe Tex and the other veterans got some sense of renewal and purpose from the hikes; they may have discovered a part of their life they left behind. (This is pure speculation on my part; Marines never talk in those terms.)

One of our early stops was at Quang Ngai, an unremarkable city well off the beaten tourist path. I'll remember it mostly for its mediocre hotel that fronted on a dry, weed-filled river bed.

The nearby village of My Lai is a place that I doubt I will ever forget. On March 16, 1968, around five hundred unarmed civilians were killed by soldiers from Charlie Company, a unit of the Americal Division. The victims were mostly old men, women, and children. The soldiers had suffered a number of recent casualties from mines and booby traps, and were on a search and destroy mission in an area known for a heavy Viet Cong presence, a place they knew by the name of Pinkville.

The Vietnamese remember this event as the Son My Massacre, but it's better known in the U.S. as the My Lai Massacre. The incident was hidden by the Army for more than a year and a half before becoming public in the fall of 1969. A number of soldiers were charged in the massacre and the subsequent cover-up, but only one man, platoon leader Lieutenant William Calley, was ever convicted. Calley was sentenced to life in prison but, thanks to the intervention of President Nixon, he was able to serve his time under house arrest. Jimmy Carter, then governor of Georgia, and many other public figures rallied to his cause. After three and a half years, he was paroled by the Secretary of the Army.

I was an intern in Dallas when the My Lai story broke. At that time, there was overwhelming support for William Calley and the soldiers at My Lai. The guerilla quagmire of Vietnam had been going on for more than four years. Month after month, hundreds of Americans were being killed in a country where everyone, young or old, male or female, was a potential enemy.

My Lai proved to be a pivotal event in the war. Many people, including those who supported the troops wholeheartedly, saw the massacre as another reason to get out of Vietnam. After *Life Magazine* published the disturbing photos from My Lai and the details of the incident slowly leaked out, public sentiment gradually changed. Vietnam became something most people wished would go away.

Today at My Lai, the facts strike you in the face; there's no way to paper over the atrocities. A museum at the entrance of the site lists the names of the five hundred and four victims on a black granite wall. (The precise number is still debated; the U.S. claims there were three hundred and forty-seven victims.) Photographs of the massacre and of the international outcry against the killings line the wall. The museum includes a tribute to Hugh Thompson, the Army helicopter pilot who spotted some of the dead and wounded civilians from the air, landed, and carried several of the villagers away to safety.

Next to the museum is a memorial statue, cast in the heroic communist style, which shows a woman holding a dead baby in one arm while the other arm thrusts a clenched fist defiantly into the air.

The several hamlets of what is collectively known as My Lai were destroyed during the massacre and later during the war. Today, there are paths leading past the foundations of some of the original buildings. The site is a patchwork of small hamlets, irrigation ditches, rice paddies, and dirt roads. One stop marks the spot where seventy to eighty villagers were pushed into an irrigation ditch and killed.

My Lai is a solemn and desolate place. Everyone in our group wandered around without uttering a word. The whole experience leaves you sad and depressed. It was even more of a shock for those not familiar with the incident. I knew what to expect, so I was stunned but not surprised. Some of the college students couldn't believe that American soldiers were capable of committing these crimes; they were incredulous when I told them of the initial strong public support for the U.S. troops.

Coming face to face with the ugly side of war is always difficult.

Later in the tour, we visited the ancient imperial city of Hue, the location of one of the fiercest battles of the entire war and the site of a horrendous massacre of innocent men, women, and children. The Battle of Hue, part of the Tet Offensive, began on the last day of January 1968 and lasted twenty-six days. The communists initially seized the entire city except for the ARVN headquarters and the American advisor compound. The country was shocked to see the Viet Cong flag flying high from the ancient Citadel at the center of the city.

The Battle for Hue was unlike any other battle during the Vietnam War. It was intense urban warfare with house-to-house fighting. The Marines entered the southern part of the city and advanced one building at a time. After crossing the Perfume River, they stormed the massive Citadel and eventually secured the Imperial Palace. The battle took nearly a month and cost more than two hundred U.S. lives.

Before they were finally driven out, the Viet Cong and North Vietnamese executed as many as five thousand people. Many were civil servants, religious leaders, and teachers. Anyone linked to the South Vietnamese cause was a target for execution. Some were bound and tortured; some may have been buried alive. The number of people killed is disputed, but few people deny that the crimes took place; the only question is the exact number of victims. Yet you won't find any mention of the Hue Massacre in the war museums of Hanoi and Ho Chi Minh City. According to today's government, the event never took place. The people of Vietnam have softened with time, but the official communist narrative of the war is rigid and unyielding, unchanged by the passage of the years.

Visiting the city today, it's easy to get a feel for the Battle of Hue. The layout of the streets is the same and many of the buildings serve the same function today as they did a half-century ago. More importantly, you can still get a real sense of the fighting by watching contemporaneous reports on YouTube. Vietnam was the first television war, cameramen and reporters were present at most of the major battles, and the fight for Hue was as big as they come.

Vietnam today, like the rest of the known world, is linked to the Internet. The small hotels, the roadside restaurants, and the neighborhood coffee shops all have Wi-Fi. I was able to view contemporaneous news reports and specials before and after my visits to the battlefields. In Hue, I watched the CBS coverage as the Marines fought to capture the city. I walked where the Marines fought, traveled the same streets, entered the same buildings, and crossed the same gates into the Citadel as the Marines once did. The Battle of Hue is a great testament to the courage and tenacity of the U.S. Marine Corps.

I had the genuine pleasure of meeting some of the Marine veterans who fought during the Battle of Hue. The encounter took place at one of my favorite places in the entire country of Vietnam, the DMZ Bar. The real DMZ is probably thirty miles north of this drinking spot, but I feel like it was close enough to justify the name. The establishment claims to have opened in 1994, around the same time as the country first opened its doors to tourism.

You can't help but like the place. The ceiling of the main room has a map of the DMZ and surrounding area. Places like Con Thien, Khe Sanh, and Camp Carroll are lit by colored lights. An inverted helicopter hangs from the ceiling, with the blades of the chopper serving as a rotating fan. The bar is far from elaborate; the room is poorly lit, and most of the light comes from the glow of neon beer signs. The floor is plain concrete, and a pool table occupies the middle of the room. The DMZ, an unpretentious drinking spot, is an easy place to get used to.

I spent a fair amount of time at the DMZ Bar, for several reasons. The menu included things like cheeseburgers and pizza, a welcome respite from the routine of rice and chopsticks three times a day. And with local beer going for less than a dollar, it was easy to get carried away by the low prices. (It's hard not to congratulate yourself for getting beer for so little money.)

The patrons were an interesting cross section. Some were part of the wandering backpacking crowd that seems to thrive on the cheap prices of Southeast Asia, while others were young Vietnamese drawn by the trappings of American culture.

Many American war veterans also frequent the DMZ Bar. The veterans were the easiest people in the world to identify—mostly white men aged sixty-five and older. Many were Marines, and quite a few had served multiple tours. They would identify the name of their unit and point out when and where they had served. We traded tales; they told me their stories and I told them mine. I rarely met a veteran who wasn't glad to talk about his time at war. As our stories unfolded, the beer seemed to come to our table like it was on autopilot. At a dollar a round, we were all generous hosts.

I like the DMZ Bar. I think that pitching the past to veterans passing through is a great idea, it's capitalism at its finest. The war caused so much death and destruction; why not turn it into today's entertainment?

To the west of Hue lies the site of a major battle. . Anyone who remembers anything at all about the Vietnam War remembers the siege of Khe Sanh. President Johnson was so concerned that the siege would result in an American defeat—one like the French suffered at Dien Bien Phu—that he had a model of the battlefield constructed in the White House. While Johnson closely followed the progress of the siege from his office in Washington, many of us at home watched daily television reports and hoped for the best.

Khe Sanh Combat Base was located in the northwest corner of South Vietnam, right below the DMZ and just ten miles from the border of Laos. The U.S. initially used Khe Sanh as a Special Forces camp, a spot from which to monitor and harass North Vietnamese troops and supplies moving down the Ho Chi Minh Trail. By late 1967, the base had been heavily reinforced and served as the western most anchor of a defensive line that ran just below the DMZ from the border of Laos to the South China Sea. Nearly seven thousand troops, mostly U.S. Marines, fought to control the hills overlooking the base.

The North Vietnamese chose Khe Sanh as the place to go on the offensive against U.S. and South Vietnamese forces, committing some twenty-seven thousand troops with artillery and tanks to the battle. The siege of Khe Sanh began on January 21, 1968, more than a week ahead of the Tet offensive. Whether Khe Sanh was a diversion to focus attention away from Tet or whether the Tet offensive was an effort to draw troops from Khe Sanh is still debated.

For seventy-seven days, the North Vietnamese pounded the combat base, dropping in an average of one hundred and fifty rounds a day. Khe Sanh was cut off from resupply by ground, the only help came by air, sometimes by parachute drops. Marines were in a dire situation, with shortages of food and water, especially at the hill outposts.

U.S. air power played a major role in turning the tide. Aided by electronic sensors that helped locate enemy troops, massive B-52 bombers were used as close air support for the first time in the war.

The North Vietnamese, as they so often did, faded away to fight another day. By April 3, the siege of Khe Sanh was over. In one of those strange and inexplicable decisions that were so common during the Vietnam War, the U.S. decided that the Khe Sanh

Combat Base really wasn't that critical and abandoned it less than two months later.

After making a stop at the Khe Sanh Combat Base on my way to Laos, I visited a second time a week later with my tour group. The base is located a few miles outside the village of Khe Sanh, in an area known for its coffee plantations. What's left of the metal-surfaced airstrip lies on a plateau surrounded by the foothill peaks that saw some of the most intense fighting of the war. A small museum portrays the siege as a heroic communist victory (both sides claim to be winners). There are some interesting examples of the seismic and acoustic sensors used by the United States, as well as exhibits of the uniforms, weapons, and kits used by both sides. Nearby is a reconstructed bunker, plus several U.S. aircraft brought in after the war. Scattered around the site are piles of spent ordnance, large metal clumps that appear to have been shaped by a frustrated sculptor.

The coffee at Khe Sanh was some of the best I've ever drunk. I enjoyed sitting in the shade outside the small gift shop drinking coffee, reflecting on the courage of U.S. Marines and talking with the local merchants. I had to be careful, though; too many questions by me would get in the way of their selling a cup of coffee and a bag of Oreos. Khe Sanh is a small place, well away from the cities, and in rural Vietnam, every source of income is valued.

TWENTY-SIX

HO CHI MINH CITY

Ho Chi Minh City was the final stop on my return trip to Vietnam. I had visited the capital of South Vietnam several times during the war, back when it was known as Saigon. The old name still hasn't disappeared; locals more often than not still call the place Saigon.

Our flight landed at Tan Son Nhut airport, once the home to the Seventh Air Force and the bustling headquarters of the air war in Southeast Asia. As we taxied to the terminal, I was immediately struck by the presence of two USAF military transport aircraft, parked in the same location they used to occupy forty-five years ago. During the war, the giant C-141 Starlifters flew for the Military Airlift Command, transporting troops and supplies around the world. The C-141s have been largely replaced by later models, but the aircraft still bear American insignia. Decades after the United States left Vietnam, the return of the USAF to Tan Son Nhut seems to have brought things full circle.

The aircraft were actually in Ho Chi Minh City as part of the advance work for President Obama's first visit to Vietnam. The President was in Hanoi when we arrived in Saigon and was due to land in Ho Chi Minh City the following day. Our guide proudly told us that Obama would be staying in a hotel right across the street from our lodging, as if the proximity to the head of state made our rooms a bit more valuable.

The Vietnamese are proud that every sitting president since Bill Clinton has visited their country. (The election of Donald Trump would come six months after my visit.) They truly value a good relationship with the United States. Mr. Obama is held in high esteem by the Vietnamese, though he appeared to have few admirers among U.S. Marine Corps veterans in my group.

The USAF aircraft on the runway at Tan Son Nhut were just one of the many ironies I encountered while traveling in Vietnam. So often during my trip, I was struck by the paradoxes of this modern nation that, despite winning the war, still seems to be in the thrall of the country they defeated.

Free market capitalism seems firmly entrenched in the communist nation of Vietnam, the country has embraced the West, and its citizens are searching for the same freedom and prosperity that the United States has long enjoyed. Today, there's a Burger King located less than a half mile from where I lived during my year at Da Nang. During the war, the Air Force mess hall's cuisine was so bland and unappealing that sometimes I had to force myself to eat; I would have paid dearly for the endless supply of Whoppers today's Vietnamese enjoy.

Each morning when I put on my shoes, either the sneakers or the leather tops, one quick glance at the label on the back of the tongue tells me that my footwear was "Made in Vietnam." I've returned to the country where I once served, but my shoes have done me one better; they have returned to their birthplace. If you are partial to American hotel chains, you can find them in nearly all the major cities. Hilton, Hyatt, Marriott, and many others provide luxury accommodations, mostly to international travelers. One night's stay probably costs more than most Vietnamese earn in a month, but the country is embracing tourism in a big way.

The 1968 Viet Cong attack on the U.S. Embassy in today's Ho Chi Minh City, one of the most significant events of the war, is commemorated by a striking monument that honors the fallen soldiers of the Tet Offensive. Tet, a military defeat for the Viet Cong, was nevertheless a major psychological blow for the United States. Millions of Americans watched as the Viet Cong breached the U.S. embassy walls. The Tet Offensive showed us that the light at the end of the tunnel was receding, rather than coming nearer.

Yet nearly a half-century later, you have to search diligently to find the monument. It's overshadowed by a giant banner advertising the local McDonald's.

The long and destructive Vietnam War was followed by an even longer decade of unadulterated communism, a failed worker's paradise. Today's Vietnamese want a better life, and they're willing to work for it.

Looking back, it sometimes seems that things would have been a lot simpler for everyone if the Vietnamese had just let us win the war.

There are few places in Vietnam that capture the spirit and the atmosphere of the war as fully as the Reunification Palace. Once the home of the President of South Vietnam, the palace fell to North Vietnamese tanks on April 30, 1975. Since that day, time has seemed to stand still at the palace. Today, it's possible to immerse yourself in a bygone era; the buildings and furnishings have been preserved much as they were at the end of the war. If Richard Nixon or Henry Kissinger dropped by, they would definitely recognize the place.

The French originally built a residence for their governor-general on the site of the current palace in the 1860s. After they were forced out in 1954 at the end of the First Indochina War, Ngo Dinh Diem, the president of the new Republic of Vietnam (South Vietnam), moved in. In 1962, the palace was bombed by members of Diem's own air force. The President ordered a new palace to be constructed on the same site and was careful to include a large bomb shelter in the new plans. Diem was assassinated in 1963 and never had a chance to live in his palace.

President Nguyen Van Thieu occupied the palace for most of the war, resigning less than two weeks before the fall of Saigon. South Vietnam's last president, Duong Van Minh (better known as Big Minh), the leader of the coup that deposed and murdered President Diem in 1963, surrendered to the communists. After the overthrow, the Presidential Palace was renamed Reunification Palace.

The palace and grounds look the same today as they did in 1971, when I first saw them on a USO tour. The whitewashed concrete building, an example of 1960s modernist architecture, was designed by a Vietnamese architect who was careful to incorporate the "feng shui" principles of balance and order. The décor and furnishings in the palace take you back to the 1960s. There are the usual staterooms, reception rooms, and living quarters, done mostly in earth tones and pastel colors; but you'll also discover rotary phones, thick plush carpets, a movie room with reels of film, a game room with a barrel-shaped bar, tennis courts, a helipad, and much more. It's the kind of place you'd see in one of the early James Bond movies.

Down in the fortress basement you'll discover hallways with map rooms and ancient-looking radio equipment. The bunkers look very similar to Winston Churchill's War Rooms in London; a veritable redoubt in a war-torn nation.

The Reunification Palace provides a sweeping overview of the rise and fall of the government of South Vietnam. The communists celebrate the collapse of the American-backed government and the reunification of the nation, but the Palace lets the facts speak for themselves. There is little of the shrill, hardline propaganda found in the communism of Stalin and Mao.

The war museums of Vietnam are another story. Visitors are ambushed at every turn by history, devoid of insight or balance and written in the bloated communist style. The vocabulary, overwrought and full of propaganda buzz words, borders on the absurd. We read of "puppets," "stooges," "henchmen," "air pirates," "imperialist war mongers," etc. These written words, the vernacular of the war, seemed to be confined to the museum. I never heard anyone use them in speech. I imagine they will eventually fade with time.

A good example of the harsh rhetoric is the War Remnants Museum in Ho Chi Minh City, one of Vietnam's most popular attractions, especially for foreign visitors. The museum opened in 1975 as the Exhibit House for U.S. and Puppet Crimes. By 1990, the Cold War had ended and the Vietnamese were struggling in a failed communist state marked by poverty and corruption. Feeling that perhaps a relationship with the capitalist West wasn't such a bad idea after all, the museum was renamed the Exhibition House for Crimes of War and Aggression. By 1995, diplomatic relations had been established between the two countries and the U.S. embargo had ended. A new sign went up: the "War Remnants Museum."

Both sides suffered during the Vietnam War; death and destruction was the common denominator. But the story of the conflict is mainly one-sided in today's museum exhibits. The War Remnants Museum in Ho Chi Minh City and the Vietnam Military History Museum in Hanoi tell the same basic story: foreign invaders—the French at first, the Americans later—occupy the country of Vietnam and terrorize the people. Communist revolutionaries, exhibiting great heroism and sacrifice and following the guidance of Uncle Ho, lead the people to victory. In Vietnam, like other communist countries, truth is a function of power; propaganda is state-controlled.

Both museums feature large amounts of captured or abandoned American military hardware, as well as a few pieces belonging to the victorious North Vietnamese. Hanoi proudly shows off a MIG-21, the major fighter aircraft of the North Vietnamese Air Force. Tank 843, which crashed the gates of the Presidential Palace in Saigon on April 30, 1975, somehow ended up in Hanoi rather than Ho Chi Minh City. A bizarre sculpture made up of pieces of wrecked U.S. aircraft occupies much of the museum courtyard in Hanoi. The symbolism is clear: the pride of American airpower, reduced to a junkyard scrap heap. The message is patriotic hyperbole at its best. LIKE YOURS

The courtyard of the War Remnants Museum in Ho Chi Minh City has its own arsenal of American military hardware. I discovered an A-37 Dragonfly similar to the one I flew in my first Air Force assignment. You can also find an F-5 fighter flown by the South Vietnamese Air Force, a Huey helicopter, and an A-1 Skyraider, plus numerous tanks, artillery pieces, and large piles of bombs, shells, and mortars. As one sign tells us, these are the instruments of war brought to wreak havoc on the peace-loving Vietnamese.

The outside is interesting, but the main message is on the inside of the museum. Agent Orange, unexploded ordnance, napalm, the My Lai Massacre, Bob Kerrey's alleged war crimes—all are prominently featured. If you somehow missed the message, there's even a guillotine used by the French to execute criminals and the "tiger cages" in which the South Vietnamese kept prisoners.

The Viet Cong and North Vietnamese soldiers play a relatively small role in the exhibits. There is no mention of their war crimes and little boasting about their military prowess. The museum is designed not to celebrate the communist victory, but to make as strong a case as possible against United States' involvement in the Vietnam War.

I was glad I visited the War Remnants Museum, in spite of its overly anti-American message. Time tends to recast most wars as patriotic and heroic endeavors; those killed and wounded are sometimes seen as mere statistics rather than flesh and blood human beings. The War Remnants Museum never lets you forget the human toll of the war.

Today's Vietnamese seem to have moved well beyond the sentiments expressed in the War Remnants Museum. The war is history; they are more interested in the future than in the past. The very same day that I visited the museum, President Obama, during his stop at Ho Chi Minh City, announced that Bob Kerrey had been appointed chairman of the American-sponsored Fulbright University Vietnam, the country's first private university. Since I had just seen a display in the War Remnants Museum accusing Bob Kerrey of war crimes, this announcement came as quite a surprise to me.

In 1969, Kerrey led a Navy SEAL team on a midnight raid on the Mekong Delta village of Than Phong, which resulted in the death of twenty unarmed Vietnamese civilians, including women and children. Less than a month later, his actions during another mission, in which he was injured and later lost the lower part of one leg, resulted in him receiving the Medal of Honor.

After the war, Kerrey enjoyed a successful business career, served as Nebraska's governor and United States senator, and even ran for president in 1992. Around 2001, the story of the Thanh Phong raid surfaced in the media, threatening to reopen old wounds from a war that both sides were trying to put behind them. Kerrey acknowledged his role in the raid and said that the incident was a tragedy that has haunted him for years.

How can a man labeled a war criminal by a nation be chosen to head one of its major universities? The Vietnamese government and people, doing their best to adopt an attitude of forgiveness and reconciliation, appear to be a few steps ahead of the museum curators. Still, time heals many, not all, wounds. Kerry's appointment generated a lot of controversy in the Vietnamese and American media, with many calling for him to be formally held accountable for his actions in Vietnam.

Unlike the My Lai Massacre, most of the Vietnamese I spoke with were unaware of the Than Phong Raid. Like many Americans, they seemed to confuse Bob Kerrey with the then-current Secretary of State John Kerry (Kerry was a naval officer who also served in the Mekong Delta area, before later joining the Vietnam Veterans Against the War).

Bob Kerrey's actions, which resulted in him receiving the Medal of Honor, speak volumes about his character and bravery. Most Vietnamese believe his devotion to the people of Vietnam is genuine and sincere and welcome his appointment.

My trip to Southeast Asia involved several in-country flights, a couple of itinerary changes, and dozens of simple problems made difficult by the need to communicate in a foreign language. Breaking through the language barrier was always a challenge, but thankfully, all through my journey I had a guardian angel of sorts looking after me.

Every few days, I would get a call from Phuong, a local Vietnamese helping me with travel arrangements. I never met Phuong (she lived in Hanoi), but she seemed devoted to making sure that things went smoothly for me. I would recognize her soft, soothing voice instantly. "John," Phuong would ask, pausing for a moment, "how was your day?" She would then carefully lay out my itinerary, give me simple, direct instructions and help me avoid the snares of foreign travel.

Phuong, a very common name in Vietnamese, is one of the main characters in the Graham Greene novel *The Quiet American*. Greene's Phuong is a beautiful Vietnamese woman who takes care of an older Westerner with skill and devotion, all the time looking after her own interests. I was glad to have a Phuong of my own to advise me while traveling around Vietnam.

Greene, already an established novelist at the time, was serving as British war correspondent in Saigon in the early 1950s when he wrote *The Quiet American*. The story is set near the end of the First Indochina War, the last gasp of French colonialism. In the novel, the two main characters, Fowler and Pyle, compete for Phuong's attention. Like many Vietnamese, Phuong is quite adaptable, able to handle whatever the war brings. Fowler, the older man, is a jaded, cynical British journalist who derides the naivety and idealism of Pyle, the titular quiet American. Pyle, a CIA operative, is searching for a better answer for Vietnam, something other than communism or colonialism, a so-called Third Force.

The Quiet American is a tangled tale of love, espionage, and murder that has twice been brought to the screen and has never been out of print. When I first read the novel in high school, it was widely viewed as anti-American. Many now view the novel as a cautionary tale that the United States chose to ignore. I remember it as a story full of moral and political ambiguities. Greene, as he often does, raised many uncomfortable questions, but provided few answers.

The Quiet American portrays the Saigon of the early 1950s. My first trip to the city came twenty years after Greene; I returned most recently another four decades later. Saigon has since become Ho Chi Minh City and the French names have given way to Vietnamese, but much of Greene's Saigon, my Saigon, is still identifiable today.

The main route, Dong Khoi, leads from the Saigon River past

the grand hotels. Though Greene spent much of his stay at the Majestic Hotel, it's the Continental Hotel that claims to be the spot where he wrote at least part of *The Quiet American.* I took the elevator to the second floor of the hotel, where a metal plaque identified room 214 as Greene's room. Much of the hotel, such as the high ceilings, old fans, and brass doorknobs, looks unchanged. Out on the street side terrace, it's another story. I remember screens of chicken wire strung on the terraces of the various hotels to protect from grenades tossed from a passing motorbike. Acts of terrorism were a daily of life during the war. Saigon is safer today, but no less exciting.

A walk past the opera house on Lam Son Square leads to Notre Dame Cathedral. Built by the French in the late 1800s, the church has a few scars from the war, but otherwise looks much the same as it did forty-five years ago. Roman Catholicism took a beating under communism, but around seven percent of the country still remains Catholic.

Walking anywhere in Ho Chi Minh City is a pleasure. It's a vibrant city in constant motion. The Vietnamese are a proud, energetic, intelligent and hard-working people. They are friendly and easy-going, respectful of their elders, and anxious to help foreigners. The war has been over for four decades, and the future looks bright for the country of Vietnam.

TWENTY-SEVEN

LOOKING BACK

RESEARCHING AND WRITING this book has been a very meaningful experience for me. I am in my seventies now, and I have an undeniable awareness of the passage of time. Sometimes it seems that somewhere along the way, I've misplaced twenty years of my life. A lot has happened in the last seven decades, but I have precious few recollections of some major events. My time in Vietnam was one of those milestones that had disappeared into the fog of life. I am happy to reach back nearly a half-century into the past and reclaim the year that I spent at Da Nang.

More than 2.5 million Americans served in the Vietnam War. When some veterans came home, the war came with them. I was fortunate; I was able to move quickly from the world of combat back into civilian life. I rarely thought about the war. I had left Vietnam and it had left me.

The general public seemed just as glad to be done with the long war. Less than a year after I left Da Nang, a peace treaty was signed and the POWs were released. America was finally finished with Vietnam.

Even though the war had been a major event in my life, I seldom had the opportunity to look back. Since few of my friends had served in the military, I was close to only a few veterans and I rarely ever crossed paths with anyone who had flown fighters in combat. My identity had changed. I was no longer a flight surgeon or an F-4 backseater. I was an ophthalmologist.

As the years slid by quickly, my recollections of Vietnam stayed mostly positive. The mind has a remarkable ability to suppress painful memories—plus, I've always been a cup half-full type of guy. Since I wasn't burdened by the war, I felt no need to romanticize or demonize the conflict. I moved on with my life, and each year the memories of Da Nang faded a bit more.

But as the fiftieth anniversary of the war approached, things changed. I began reading and remembering, looking at old photographs, talking with other veterans, rummaging through forgotten letters I had written from Vietnam. Anniversaries give us a reason to reminisce, an excuse to delve into the past. My interest in the conflict grew; the personal experiences of other veterans became more interesting to me. When I encountered a patient in my office who had served in the war, I had to hear his story. More than anything, attending my fighter wing reunion made my days in Vietnam come back alive. Many of the things I did at Da Nang now took on a clarity and a meaning that were absent during my tour.

When I left Vietnam, I had no mixed emotions; I was happy to be done. I had no desire to ever come back. But if you are wise, you try to learn from your past. I am a richer man for having revisited my year in Vietnam and I'm a better person for having returned to a country that I yearned to leave from the very first day I arrived.

I'm probably not unique. For most people who went to Southeast Asia, their military service was a defining moment in their life. Regardless of your role in the conflict, you saw a lot of things that you'd never seen before. The Vietnam War was a poorly-conceived, ill-defined conflict fought on the other side of the planet. Some people drew a better lot than others, but everyone, to a certain extent, was in the same boat. We were all plucked from the safety and prosperity of American life and dropped into a land of poverty and violence. There was a sense of unity, togetherness, and shared adversity. You became part of a brotherhood of Vietnam veterans.

Wartime elevated the experience of each day. Serving in Vietnam had a perverse attraction; life became brighter, more intense, and more meaningful when you introduced the risk of losing it. Life was more fragile, injury and death could arrive quickly, nothing was definite. Being forced to confront fear and accept the challenges of combat also brought certain rewards. If all went as planned, your fear gave way to courage and the sense of being fully alive. For me, Vietnam was a lifetime of high drama concentrated in one year, a great adventure that was fascinating, frightening, and fulfilling.

Flying in an F-4 Phantom raised the stakes greatly, but it also increased the rewards. The possibility of failure—getting shot down, killed, or imprisoned—made the eventual success that much more gratifying. Each combat mission brought a sense of happiness and relief that came from accepting a dangerous challenge and having had the strength to endure. The relief always far outweighed the satisfaction.

In life, the people you meet along the way are what give your journey its shape and color. I still see fighter pilots in a bold, vivid way: intelligent men, skilled and courageous, who acted gracefully in the face of danger. These men had a sense of adventure and preferred action to reflection; they were exactly who they claimed to be. I flew only a fraction of the missions that the regular F-4 crews flew, but it was more than enough to appreciate their valor and sense of duty.

When I first came to Da Nang, I was unsure of my role in the squadron. As a flight surgeon, there were few rules to guide me. I was an outsider, a man who brought little to the table other than a desire to be part of the team. The idea of flying combat missions in a fighter was a little vague and outlandish, but full of promise and mystery. My squadron generously included me in its missions, I was recognized as one of the boys by the boys themselves. I always considered the opportunity to fly as more of a reward than a duty.

Looking back, it's easy to be romantic about the Vietnam War, but it's even easier to be a little cynical. By the time I came to Da Nang in 1971, the irrationality of the conflict was already apparent. It had been a long, bloody six years, and the war had been pushed to the backburner by American society. The ground war was winding down, and peace with honor was alleged to be just around the corner. The air war continued, but the rules of engagement had eliminated any real chance of victory.

Today, there's little that everyone can agree on about the Vietnam War. The motives of the United States for intervening in Vietnam were exemplary. We went to Southeast Asia for the purpose of containing communism, our efforts made with the best of intentions. Communism was no imaginary threat; under Stalin and Mao, tens of millions of people had been beaten, starved, or worked to death, if not outright killed. The Cold War was real and the Vietnam War, much like the Korean conflict, was a difficult-to-avoid proxy war. Although the United States, fighting for a good cause beside a weak, corrupt ally, eventually prevailed in the Cold War, the postponement of the communist takeover in Vietnam came at a high price.

Looking back today, it's easy to see how our country became mired in an unwinnable war. From the start, the conflict was burdened with numerous heavy-handed restrictions and poorly-defined military objectives that made military victory, at least in the usual sense of the word, impossible to achieve. Initially, everyone seemed to agree that North Vietnam was the enemy and that the communists had to be prevented from taking over South Vietnam. Yet President Johnson's response was a weak Rolling Thunder air campaign with a gradual escalation and frequent pauses, a strategy that proved to be ineffective. Because of the fear of Chinese or Soviet intervention, no invasion of North Vietnam was permitted. The North had an agrarian economy that depended on supplies from their communist allies that came mostly by ship through the port of Haiphong, but until 1972, the harbor was off-limits to bombing or mining. Although most of the men and materiel from North Vietnam traveled south via the Ho Chi Minh Trail in Laos, U.S. troops were forbidden from entering the country in any significant numbers.

Anyone serving in the military prefers a war with clear and tangible goals. Our strategy in Vietnam was to try and convince the enemy that they couldn't win. The North Vietnamese never got the message.

The United States involvement in Vietnam mostly ended by 1973. Our POWs came home, and our nation was glad to end a painful chapter in our history. There were no drum rolls or fanfare; the public had long ago stopped being emotionally involved in the conflict.

Nearly a half-century later, an honest reckoning shows that the bad far outweighed the good. What remains is a terrible sense of waste; a tragedy for both sides. The fifty-eight thousand U.S. deaths; the many thousands wounded; the men still MIA; the millions of Vietnamese killed and wounded; the legacy of Agent Orange and unexploded ordnance…

War has the ability to make fools of everyone.

I consider myself lucky to have spent a year in Vietnam. I was fortunate enough to fight the war mostly from high in the sky, shielded from the possibility of human contact. Down below, Americans were killed and wounded. The Vietnamese on both sides fought, reproduced, suffered, and died. I was the fortunate son, I went home after a year and left the war in Vietnam.

In those twelve months, I accumulated a lifetime of experiences. I learned more about service, sacrifice, and camaraderie than I have ever learned. Vietnam showed me the reality of war, it left me less innocent, more aware of the imperfect world we live in and its flawed leaders.

It's often difficult to make sense of life in a war zone. Why do some people die and some people live? War gives life in so many ways, but it more often takes it away. The great losses of the conflict cast a certain shadow over the Vietnam War, but they do not diminish the bravery and courage of the men who served. I have only praise and regret for those lives cut short. I honor their sacrifice.

ACKNOWLEDGMENTS

THE YEARS HAVE blurred, altered, and erased many of my memories of Vietnam. While researching and writing this book, I sometimes found that things I once thought to be true were incorrect. Since facts can grow murkier with the passage of time, I have relied on objective, contemporaneous sources as much as possible in writing this book, resisting the urge to reinvent my year at Da Nang.

Living in a foreign land away from the people you love is the worst part of going to war. Since there was no telephone or internet, the most important part of my day at Da Nang was mail call. During my year in Vietnam I wrote more than one hundred and fifty letters—mostly to my wife, but also to my mother. Both of them were wise enough to keep those letters, something that I failed to do on my end. My letters home capture many of the details of my tour at Da Nang and provide an accurate account of my feelings about the war.

When I left the Air Force, I kept a copy of my flight records that covers all but my last month at Da Nang. My career as an F-4 Phantom backseater is there in black and white. I can tell when I flew, to a certain extent where I went, how long the sortie lasted, and even the tail number of the aircraft I flew in. Unfortunately, the name of the pilot in the front seat is not part of the record.

Many of these men I remember well, others I recall by their first name only; some are simply a nameless face.

The Gunfighters, the men of the 366th TFW, helped me in so many ways. I thank them for including me in their circle. The 366th TFW has a long and distinguished history dating back to World War II. The wing holds an annual reunion, attended mostly by veterans of the Vietnam conflict. These gatherings were a valuable source of background information about life at Da Nang. I was able to clarify and confirm many of the details of my year in Vietnam. If enough people remember something from the past in the same way, it is probably true. If I asked a dozen men something, such as the location of the mess hall, and all twelve told me that it was just opposite the dispensary, I could be sure that that detail was correct.

I conducted more than thirty interviews with fighter pilots, backseaters, and other men involved in fighting the war. Quite a few of them spent a career in the Air Force and are experts in various aspects of aviation. I was able to relearn many of the finer points of flying as a GIB in an F-4 in combat, and I also picked up much that I never knew. When I left Da Nang, I left flying completely. Since Vietnam, all of my time in the air has been spent as a passenger in commercial aircraft. I honestly feel that there has never been anyone who logged more than fifty combat missions in a fighter aircraft who knows less about flying than I do.

Since I'm no expert on flying, I've tried to keep descriptions as simple as possible. I've used miles per hour (mph) rather than the more commonly employed nautical miles (knots). Instead of talking about pounds of fuel used by an aircraft, I have spoken in gallons.

No one forgets a war they were part of. Over 2.5 million people served in Vietnam, and each one of them has a story; most are anxious to share their experiences. I received help from many sources at every stage of researching and writing this book.

A special thanks goes to Joe Dunaway and his family. Joe had a distinguished career as a USAF fighter pilot, including a year with the 4th TFS at Da Nang. He volunteered and was chosen for the Stormy Fast FAC program, one of the most dangerous challenges a fighter pilot can face. Joe helped me understand much of what I did as a GIB. He was kind enough to answer endless questions about flying, as well as taking the time to review parts of my book. His wife Dotty and his son Brian gave me valuable insights into the challenges the family of a fighter pilot faces.

I owe a special debt to Ken Dahl, a man who spent much of his Air Force career in the backseat of an F-4 Phantom. Ken helped me remember where all the buttons, switches, knobs, levers, tubes, wires, and such were located in the rear cockpit. After talking with Ken, I was better able to reconstruct the details of my duties as a GIB.

I want to thank Dori Bond LeBlanc for sharing the story of the loss in combat of her brother Ron. Dori had just turned seventeen and returned home with her first driver's license when she learned that her older brother, who she adored, was MIA. Ron's remains have never been found. She and her family have lived for decades without knowing exactly what happened on September 30, 1971.

Mahlon Long was kind enough to describe the details of his rescue from the Ho Chi Minh Trail in Laos. Long's OV-10 aircraft was shot down just prior to the launch of the Easter Offensive in 1972. He was saved from certain death or captivity by the brave SAR crews who flew and manned the Sandys and the Jolly Green rescue helicopters. I knew him as an A-37 pilot in my first Air Force assignment and was surprised and delighted to see him once again on his return to Da Nang after a successful rescue.

I am indebted to Ed "Tex" Stiteler and his organization, Vietnam Battlefield Tours, for helping me learn about the ground war in Vietnam. Tex is a decorated Marine Corps veteran who was wounded in action while serving in Vietnam from 1966–1967. He later joined with several other veterans to form a non-profit organization dedicated to providing reasonably-priced and professionally-staffed tours of the battlefields of Southeast Asia. I never had to face the dangers and challenges that the men in the field encountered. I give thanks for their courage and sacrifice.

I thank Sara Priebe for once again, as she did with my first book, providing excellent maps to accompany my story. As a backseater in an F-4, I spent a lot of time before, during, and after each mission scrutinizing maps. This may have been where I first developed the almost compulsive need to know where I am whenever I leave home. I've always felt there should be a law against publishing a history or travel book without maps. Sara's skillful work should help everyone better understand the terrain of Southeast Asia.

In spite of an opening night rocket attack, my first days at Da Nang went relatively smoothly, thanks in large part to Jim Rooks. Jim, the flight surgeon for the 390th TFS, rotated home a couple of weeks after I arrived. He set a high standard, both as a physician and an F-4 GIB, which made my transition much easier. I have enjoyed reestablishing contact with him after forty-five years.

I want to thank Sarah Atkinson for helping me prepare this manuscript for publication. She responded promptly to numerous deadlines and made my job a lot easier.

Once again, the professional team at Hatherleigh Press has helped guide me through the long process of writing and publishing this book. Andrew Flach, Ryan Tumambing, and Anna Krusinski assisted me at every turn. I am especially grateful for the work of my editor, Ryan Kennedy. His advice greatly improved this book.

Finally, I want to thank my wife Polly and my three children, John, Eric, and Patricia, for their love and support.